BOOK ACKNOWLEDGMENTS

Terri Levine's latest book *Turbocharge Your Business* is the perfect guide for any business owner who is conscious, spiritual and wants to run a business based on authenticity, integrity, and transparency.

—Michael Bernard Beckwith
Founder - Agape international Spiritual center
Author - Life Visioning Process

Tired of business as usual? Want to operate from your heart AND make money doing so? Dr. Terri Levine shows you how inside *Turbocharge Your Business*."

—Linda Stirling
Thepublishingcircle.com

Just when I thought I had 'learned it all' after reading Terri's a-mazing book, *Turbocharge*, here she is with an updated, content rich follow up with her latest publication: *Turbocharge Your Business!* In two days I read it cover to cover. I'm now in the process of highlighting, making new plans and digesting her invaluable knowledge to put solid ideas into action. This woman has the audacity to be considered as a #1 business strategist and has definitely earned her right. Really serious about growing your business? Then align with a serious mentor.

—Bonnie Ross-Parker, aka, America's Connection Diva/Author/
Speaker/Founder of *Xperience Connections*

This book gives you the core strategies needed to turbocharge your business. Its strategies are critical to any business owner's success. The principles in *Turbocharge Your Business* can double or even triple your business if executed. Get this book and follow the proven steps! You'll be glad you did!

The strategies outlined in Terri Levine's *Turbocharge Your Business* have helped create 7 figure businesses for both myself and my clients. Follow the steps and get Turbocharged!

—*Ben Gay III "The Closers" series*

In *Turbocharge Your Business,* Terri Levine walks you through her process of how to create a thriving business without begging for clients or selling. She explains it in great detail with actionable steps and brilliant case studies that leave you feeling both energized and relieved knowing you can succeed without efforting any longer. If you've ever felt overwhelmed, frustrated or burned out, this book will show you the way out. It is a "must-read" for every entrepreneur who is ready to build a heart-centered, no-pressure business.

—*Ellen Violette*
Creator of the Bestseller Business Blueprint
www. bestsellerbusinessblueprint.com

If you've been struggling with how to make social networks work for you to grow your business, here's the must-read book for you. Terri not only provides step-by-step strategies, she shares before and after stories of those who have successfully implemented these techniques. Open the pages of *Turbocharge Your Business* and get fired up!

—*Debra Jason*
Author of Millionaire Marketing On A Shoestring Budget

TURBOCHARGE YOUR BUSINESS

By Dr. Terri Levine

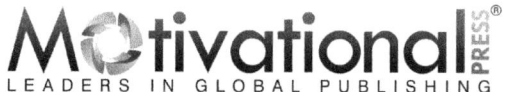

Published by Motivational Press, Inc.
1777 Aurora Road
Melbourne, Florida, 32935
www.MotivationalPress.com

Copyright 2018 © by Terri Levine
All Rights Reserved

No part of this book may be reproduced or transmitted in any form by any means: graphic, electronic, or mechanical, including photocopying, recording, taping or by any information storage or retrieval system without permission, in writing, from the authors, except for the inclusion of brief quotations in a review, article, book, or academic paper. The authors and publisher of this book and the associated materials have used their best efforts in preparing this material. The authors and publisher make no representations or warranties with respect to accuracy, applicability, fitness or completeness of the contents of this material. They disclaim any warranties expressed or implied, merchantability, or fitness for any particular purpose. The authors and publisher shall in no event be held liable for any loss or other damages, including but not limited to special, incidental, consequential, or other damages. If you have any questions or concerns, the advice of a competent professional should be sought.

Manufactured in the United States of America.

ISBN: 978-1-62865-553-7

CONTENTS

DEDICATION 7
ACKNOWLEDGMENTS 8
FOREWORD 10
INTRODUCTION 12

CHAPTER ONE
THE EXPANDED HEART-REPRENEUR® PHILOSOPHY 19

MORE OPPORTUNITY TO CONNECT THAN EVER BEFORE 20
BECOME THE CELEBRITY IN YOUR FIELD WITH EASE 37
MONKEY MIND YOU NO LONGER CONTROL ME -
I'M IN CHARGE NOW! 59

CHAPTER TWO
LEAVE THE PAST IN THE PAST 81

FORGET EVERYTHING YOU KNOW ABOUT SALES
AND MARKETING RIGHT NOW! 82
STOP USING TRADITIONAL MARKETING MEDIA 105
STOP TRYING TO CONVERT PEOPLE 112

CHAPTER THREE
MAKE IT FUN, EASY, AND EFFORTLESS...............................119

    SET UP FREEDOM SYSTEMS 120
    LEVERAGE AND AUTOMATE EVERYTHING.......................124
    THE RIGHT PEOPLE CONVERT THEMSELVES 128

CHAPTER FOUR
SHOW AND TELL 141

    GIVE PEOPLE PRACTICAL VALUE................................142
    POSITIONING THAT'S MYSTERIOUS AND EXCITING 149
    ALLOW PEOPLE TO TRY YOUR BEST, RISK FREE.................159
    PREEMINENCE 174

CHAPTER FIVE
MAGNETIZE YOUR GROUP 179

    BE THE AUTHORITY IN YOUR FIELD 180
    MOVE FROM A GENERALIST TO A CELEBRITY 185

    CONCLUSION 201

    ABOUT THE AUTHOR 204

DEDICATION

This book is dedicated to my client family members. I am so honored to be your mentor and friend. You have opened your heart and allowed me into your businesses and lives. You allow me to share my gifts with you and we are partners on this journey. I am deeply honored you have selected me and trust me to guide your business forward.

I am blessed to have the most brilliant clients on the planet who are truly Heart-repreneurs and who pass forward what I share with them to serve their client family members. I could not make the difference I am making in this world without you!

When I was 17 years old I wrote this in one of my journals having no idea what this meant at the time. "I want to impact people all over the world. I want to help others and to be of service. I want to share with people and engage with them on a very deep level and in a very profound way".

I know the work I am doing is for the greater good and send you love, light, and blessings for being part of my client family, and creating a world filled with Heart-reprenur® based businesses.

I love you,

T

ACKNOWLEDGMENTS

I have had so many amazing mentors on my journey who have helped me grow both personally and professionally and who have sculpted my success.

My first mentor was the great Zig Ziglar, who got me excited about changing lives as I changed my own.

As I entered the field of coaching and consulting many decades ago, Thomas Leonard was a mentor and friend who I learned my coaching skills from and who directly impacted my success in the coaching world.

My friend and mentor Joe Vitale, I am so honored to have co-authored a book with you in the past and now to have you write the foreword for this book. I am grateful and honored.

Scott Hallman, thank you for adding to my knowledge of business growth success ideas.

Mark Victor Hansen, the people I met as a result of knowing you and the ideas you gave me about writing really have shaped a lot of my decisions.

Michael Tasner, you turned me onto Jay Conrad Levinson, and got me going as a Master Certified Guerrilla Marketing Trainer and Coach. The two books I co-authored with Jay came because of you. You are a friend and key business and marketing strategist to me.

Joel Bauer, YOU are the mentor who has been my friend and the person who has guided my financial success as well as ability to deeply impact audiences of thousands and thousands of people as I speak around the world. My gratitude for you is beyond words and I consider you the absolute number one mentor who has shaped my income.

Frank Kern, you are one of the greatest marketers I've ever known. I am inspired by your ideas, your talents, and your ability to share what you know and give content away so freely. Because of your teachings, I've been able to create more goodwill with my own audience, and help my clients to shift their thinking and create goodwill-based businesses.

Justin Sachs, thank you for sculpting my business over the past few years, supporting all my book ideas, and expanding my ability to touch so many lives. I love working with you as a business strategist as well as having you as my publisher. It is a delight to work with you and to be part of the Motivational Press family.

Jack Canfield, I've learned so much from you about the principles of life success and they have become my daily rituals. You are doing great work in the world.

This book is dedicated to my client family members who have allowed me to embrace, nurture, and to take them under my wings. I love you.

FOREWORD

Let me ask you a few questions:

How much more money do you want to make this year?

What if I told you I know a proven way to accomplish that goal?

What if I told you it is simple and direct, too?

And what if I told you it is revealed in these pages?

Would you drop everything, devour this book, and take notes along the way?

You are in for a treat. Not only is this book brilliant but also fun. It's breezy and easy and yet contains great depth. You can read it in an evening and implement new money-attracting ideas the same evening. I wrote down insights as I read, and I've been in marketing more than thirty years. I found new ways of acting and thinking from these pages, new ways to attract prospects and money, and you will, too.

The reason you'll get so much is the author. She's a gem. I've known her about twenty years. I've seen her generate more income from more sales faster than virtually anyone I've ever met. Her secret is in coming from her heart while also following a strategy that works. In other words, she is heart-centered with an eye on the bottom line. No wonder she coined the phrase The Heart-repreneur® approach. The name says it all: an entrepreneur with heart. That's Terri Levine.

Another reason you'll love this book is due to its pathfinder mentality. Terri knows many old methods of marketing and selling are now prehistoric. There's a new customer on the block. This new breed of buyer wants to be addressed differently; with love, focus, and respect. As Terri proves, when you target the right buyer, and speak to that buyer's desires, you will rake in money – almost so easily that you'll chuckle at the simplicity of it. She's created a new path to do just that.

For example, Terri offers one question – and only one question – that alone will call out your buyers. All you need is the one specific question. With it, you can unlock a vault of riches. That's the power of the right question. And you'll find it in the first chapter of this marvelous book.

Another thing you'll find that is worth millions of dollars is a proven strategy. I learned decades ago that you need a step-by-step plan to succeed. A formula. A process. A code. Sometimes you have to stumble in the dark and invent a plan. But other times – like today – you'll find one that works that is spelled out for you. It's in this book, and it is worth gold.

Terri also reveals how to use social media, such as Facebook, to attract new prospects. But she does it without paying Facebook or running ads. Her approach is free, based on being attentive to people, and leveraging the no cost services of Facebook. In other words, she shows you how to get Facebook to bring you more business. Brilliant, right? You'll find that in chapter two.

I could go on and on with all the cool ideas, tips, tricks, techniques and strategies Terri offers in this revised and updated edition of her amazing book. But I don't want to keep you from the book, or from making money from your implementing what you learn in these pages. So I'll bow out and let Terri take the stage.

Get out your notebook and your highlighter and prepare to be amazed.

Dr. Joe Vitale
Author of way too many books to list here.
www.MrFire.com

INTRODUCTION

I have made a unique discovery. I have figured out a way to grow my business, and the businesses of other people, in an easy and effortless way. This has resulted in more profitability and more fun in my business.

I decided to share this concept with more people. I knew that if I wrote this book, you would have an opportunity to hold this book in your hands. I offer you the opportunity to achieve the same successes that my clients and I have achieved.

I've been in business for many years. At the beginning of owning my first business, it was a great struggle. I was doing traditional marketing. I spent a lot of money. I could reach general audiences, but not my target audience. I felt really frustrated.

I was trying to:

» Make money
» Bring clients on board
» Provide services
» Do the marketing

At the same time, I felt the financial stress of not having enough clients.

Over the years, I threw out everything I had ever learned about marketing and selling because all that I had learned caused me stress. I decided to invent my own process that would be fun, and one that allowed me to be authentic and connect with my target audience through my heart as a *Heart-repreneur®*.

When I took this approach, all of a sudden it was easy for me to get clients—not just any clients, but the *right* clients. In fact, when I started my mentoring business, I had thirty clients in thirty days, and I've never looked back. I don't do any conventional selling; I leverage and optimize everything, and the right people show up. They not only make my business profitable, but more importantly, they also make it fun and allow me to do the work that I love.

I feel so blessed with my business, and I want to share this blessing with you.

I wrote this book to get what I know right into your hands, and I'm glad that you've picked it up.

You have the chance to do what I've done:

- » Enjoy your business more than ever before
- » Achieve what you want in your business
- » Overcome any limitations
- » Create your business *your* way

It has been a joy to write this particular book. Although I've authored many books over the years, I've struggled with some; others have taken years to write, and only this book has been easy and effortless for me to write.

What is the difference?

The difference is how much passion I have for sharing the content to help other's in business achieve what my clients and I have been able to achieve.

Introduction

My heart opened while I was writing this book. I held nothing back. In the process of writing, I have treated my readers as if they were my highest-paid clients, as if I were sitting right there with them building their businesses.

I have a deep desire to help others get where they want to be, and to do it in a joyful and effortless way. Writing this book was natural: I was fully focused on you and your experience.

I wanted to make this somewhat of a keepsake, a reference text. I wanted to write a book that people would refer to over and over again. After writing this book, I was actually sad that I wasn't going to be able to engage the reader any further. I wanted to nurture and embrace the reader even more. I really poured out my heart.

Right now, as you're reading these words, know that my heart is with you as we embark on this journey together.

I encourage you to grab some colored pens and maybe even some highlighters as you read. I want you to write in this book—make sure that you underline, circle, highlight, star anything that resonates with you, anything you might want to read again. I want you to really engage with, get close to it.

I think many of us were taught that writing in our books is disrespectful, but I'm going to encourage you to make this a messy book in terms of all the notes and colors you can make to remind you of the most important ideas, strategies, tools, lessons, and tips that I'm sharing. It's okay—I give you full permission to mark it up, fold pages, and take notes in the margins.

When I read books like this one before, I was always afraid to mark them up. Now I've learned that when I mark up my books, it helps me remember what I need to know, and it gives me the opportunity to quickly recapture what I need to know without having to re-read the whole book.

Go ahead and grab your colored pens and highlighters, because we're going to build your business together using this book, starting right now.

Introduction

No matter where you are in your business at this moment—whether you are extremely successful, or struggling, or just doing okay—there's one thing that I know; you can feel more at ease, experience more joy, and advance your business further when you work as a Heart-repreneur®.

I'm not suggesting that the way you're doing business is wrong. I'm simply suggesting there's a way to do it more efficiently, and more from your heart. As you're reading these words, I want you not only to take the tools and techniques into your heart, but I want you to apply them. My goal is to provide you with the most practical, results-oriented book that improves all aspects of your business.

This book can be a complete game-changer for the way that you do business. It takes your success far beyond what you've achieved in the past.

As you're reading the book, I want you to visualize that you have more:

- » Income
- » Sales
- » Revenue
- » Profits

And I picture you having all of this with ease.

I see you having the ideal clients, having no struggle in your business, and being empowered—breakthrough after breakthrough—to grow your business in a heartfelt way. By the time you finish reading the book and following the suggestions, I'm confident that you will have made significant improvements in your business in an easy, effortless way, using the revolutionary process that I'm sharing full-on with you.

My goal is to transform your business. I consider it a great honor to be able to share my material with you.

You may wonder why I decided to revise *Turbocharge*. When I wrote the first edition of *Turbocharge* I shared my unique discovery of how to

Introduction

grow a business, any business, in an easy and effortless way. I gave all the secrets of how I had built my own businesses and my clients businesses to be super profitable while allowing fun and freedom in our lives.

During the past year, I discovered some new techniques and strategies that are skyrocketing my own business and that my clients are raving about. I've heard from a lot of my consulting clients using the same phrasing which is, "I wish you had put this idea in *Turbocharge*". When I heard the same thing more than 16 times, I finally realized I needed to share this new knowledge to propel your business forward even faster.

Clients show up every day to hire me because they don't have enough leads, they don't know how to convert the leads they do have, they are struggling to make a profit, or are overwhelmed and working a lot of hours on content creation. Some have a lot of clients and aren't being paid a lot of money, others are sick and tired of marketing, and others hate the idea of selling.

Which category do you fit into?

For each category, you will find the answers you seek inside these pages.

The other reason I am compelled to revise *Turbocharge* is because I now have embraced over 2,600 people since writing the first edition who have joined my Heart-repreneur® Movement and I want to continue to impact the world with this concept and nurture thousands of business owners to do business with authenticity, integrity and transparency.

The world is a bit chaotic right now with politics and terrorists and with all this uncertainty we can at least have stability in our work and bring our services and products to the world by learning to do business with heart, even though there is unrest.

This revision is my way of paying it forward and I still believe what I learned from Zig Ziglar back in 1982, "You can have everything in life you want, if you will just help other people get what they want." I am here to help you get more of what you do want in your business and your life and this revised edition of *Turbocharge* will do just that.

The new and expanded content is going to really help you progress in your business and you will be grateful to have the tools, tips, and techniques I have added.

My mission is large. I want to see a world where business owners truly love their clients and treat them as extended family. Where they deeply appreciate their vendors, and where they honor, respect and celebrate their employees.

It is time for transformation and to move away from information. Every revision is going to assist you to easily make shifts in your business that will pay off, literally pay off.

I also want you to consider me your mentor on this journey as we amp up your business together.

You may be a new business, a thriving business, an expanding, growing business or even a struggling business. It doesn't matter. When you get on board as a Heart-repreneur® you will have the tools you need to do business from a gentle, loving place that will bring you results beyond your expectations. I feel confident saying this as that's what my clients report to me.

My purpose in this revision is to get you real, concrete, measurable results that you are delighted with. Take a moment and think about what is working and going right in your business. What makes those things work?

Now jot down your ideal vision of what you want your business to look like, feel like, sound like, taste like, smell like - yes, even smell and taste! Take time to breathe life into your business before you read another page. I'm serious. After mentoring over 5,000 business owners for many decades, I know what works.

After you have your ideal vision written down in Technicolor, I want you to think about what is not quite right yet in your business. Jot that down. And finally, what tools or resources do you need to improve your business? This exercise will ground you for the journey that is about to begin!

Introduction

Are you ready for takeoff? Are you going to allow less struggle and more ease into your business and your life? If so, then go ahead and turn the page and let's play in this energy to impact more people. As I help you serve those you bring results and outcomes to, we are connected in the energy of expanding heart-to-heart businesses everywhere.

I want you to really engage, get close to it and use it as your business bible for at least twelve months.

With the additional material I have included in *Turbocharge Your Business* you will get the results my clients are getting and that is why I wrote this book for YOU!

CHAPTER ONE

• • • • • • • • • •

THE EXPANDED
HEART-REPRENEUR® PHILOSOPHY

MORE OPPORTUNITY TO CONNECT THAN EVER BEFORE

There are so many ways to connect with people without having to hunt or fish for them these days. The days of advertising and spending a lot of money to find qualified leads are over. As long as your product or service creates a genuine outcome and results for the people who purchase it you can ethically and honestly market to prospects who are anxious, excited, and ready to receive the gifts your business provides.

Just as I said in the first edition of *Turbocharge*, you don't need to use hype, false claims, sell, manipulate, and pressure people into purchasing or to spend time overcoming sales objections. Those days are over if you follow the processes I share that work for me and for my clients.

You can reach the people who are looking for the results you offer, as long as you are clear that what you are selling actually provides them with the outcome they are seeking.

Today, we can have a sales process that's easier and more efficient. It can:

» Generate more revenue and increase our customer base

» Be easy and effortless

- Deliver a great experience to our customers even *before* they purchase from us

HERE'S WHAT WE DON'T NEED TO DO:
- Rely on hype or false claims
- Overcome objections
- Pressure people into purchasing

We have the tremendous opportunity, the best that we've ever had in the history of civilization, to reach people using the internet. This great tool is where thousands of people can see us, connect with us, and choose us. It's truly a blessing and a gift.

People buy for two reasons: they want to achieve a goal or they want to solve a problem in their business or their life. So, they are ready to buy as long as you know the exact problem they want solved or goal they want achieved. You cannot guess at this.

Since the first edition of *Turbocharge,* I discovered a question that I now ask prospects and clients that allowed me to know what they wanted and to serve them better. I have all my clients use this same question and ask prospects and clients on social media, by email and by survey tools such as Surveymonkey or Google Forms.

Here is the exact question to use, "If I can only give you ONE result, what result or outcome would you want me to give you?". I did this myself and the answer gave me insight so that I actually changed the name of my program based upon the responses I got. My six-week program was called Master Class and my clients and prospects told me they wanted to learn how to attract high paying clients who loved them. Boom! Program name changed to: *The Ultimate System to Attract High Paying Clients Who Love You* (https://www.heart-repreneur.com/master-class). Once I changed the name I easily attracted 17 new members into the program. Why? I understood the result my audience wanted and I simply offered a program giving them the result and the title of the program told them that.

Now, do you want to know how I reached my target audience at ZERO cost?

REACH MILLIONS FOR NO OR LITTLE COST

Going beyond what I wrote in the first edition of *Turbocharge*, we are blessed today to be able to use even more online tools to reach qualified prospects who are seeking the results and outcomes we provide.

Most businesses use the internet in a very transactional way. The Heart-repreneur® approach, on the other hand, really calls out to your ideal target audience and allows them to connect with you. They begin to get to know you, to like you and to trust you. Instead of marketing at them and selling to them you make connections that are based on creating value and educating qualified prospects so they can get excited about achieving their results or having their problems solved.

In fact, you can become the leading expert in your niche when you decide to reach people heart to heart, creating value for them. Just as I stated in the first edition of *Turbocharge*, "You can rise to the top of your industry and dominate the market—that is, if you market with heart, and if you market by turning your prospects on rather than turning them off."

Today, people are leery of hype and claims. They are sick and tired of paying false experts who aren't able to deliver what they claim. You will stand out in your field as the go-to expert if you are authentic, in integrity, and transparent. You no longer need to do expensive marketing that doesn't work and is transactional. You can stop any direct mail and cold calling.

The way that I am filling all my programs (while I sleep!) and teaching my client family members to do the same thing is about to be revealed to you. If you follow what I am about to tell you, the power to quickly attract a ton of qualified prospects is in your hands!

Are You Ready?

I pick something educational that will serve my ideal clients - some knowledge they seek or skill they need. I know what they want because I asked them the question I shared with you. As a reminder, the question is, "If I can help you achieve just one outcome or result, what result or outcome would you want?"

I send an email out to my list about what I am going to share, let them know I will be teaching on Facebook Live the next day, tell them the exact time and date, and give them the link to the page where I will be broadcasting from. I also post that same information the day before I go live to my Facebook pages, ie: (https://www.facebook.com/HeartrepreneurTerriLevine) and all of the Facebook groups I manage, ie: (https://www.facebook.com/groups/heartrepreneurswithterrilevine/)

Then, one hour before I go live, I send a reminder to my email list, create another post on Facebook reminding them I am going live, the topic I will be teaching, and the link to the page I will be live on. I make sure the result I am teaching is something they really want.

I get on the Facebook Live and I give value, value and more value. I encourage them to like, love, wow, comment and share and I interact with their comments. I stay on live as if I am teaching a webinar sharing a ton of content for about 30 minutes. Yes, you heard me right, 30 minutes. Why 30 minutes? It takes Facebook time to build you an audience. The longer you are on (I've found 30 minutes is perfect), the more of your target audience views your live broadcast.

So, how does this translate into clients? I tell people they can direct message me on Facebook with questions or comments or to receive a 10-minute game plan session with me. I also notice who is very interactive and if those people don't message me, I message them, offer some help and a game plan session.

I must share this with you before I continue... as I am writing this information for you, a client messaged me on Facebook. She told me she just watched a health coach who did a Facebook live and she commented on it. She then said that a few minutes after the live he kept messaging her trying to sell her and she was incredibly turned off! That's my point!

Message people NOT to sell them. Message to connect, to serve, and to help, with no attachment to the outcome. This is how a Heart-repreneur® does business. We help. We educate. We give.

To me, this is the essence of what a Heart-repreneur® is, and this is the core of our philosophy. We don't need to be pushy, we don't need to sell, we don't manipulate, we don't struggle to get in front of people.

Instead, we look at how we can serve people. What do they really want and really need that we can provide? What are they seeking on social media? What are they talking about?

We look at our clients' and our prospects social media to find their pain and their goals. What do they want more of? What do they want less of? Then, we use Facebook Live to deliver high value information and watch the qualified leads pour in!

Because of the advances of the internet, there is an enormous amount of competition, but we can embrace that. Competition is actually a good thing. The internet opens up more awareness and ability for us to sort through and find who we resonate and connect with.

Our potential clients can do the same thing; they can get a sense of competitors who are not truly coming from the heart, but are really looking at people and their businesses in more of a transactional approach. This side-by-side comparison gives Heart-repreneurs a real advantage.

As a Heart-repreneur®, you have the ability to reach so many potential consumers or clients. You can rise to the top of your industry and dominate the market—that is, *if* you market with heart, and if you market by turning your prospects on, rather than turning them off. You will be moving away from high pressure sales, hype, and big claims. You're moving toward marketing in an easy and effortless way that reflects your integrity.

One of the biggest problems over the years has been the expense of marketing. Another is looking for or finding your customers.

It used to be that to find your audience you had to:

» Rely on direct mail
» Spend a lot of time going to networking meetings
» Buy lists for mailings or cold calls

The internet and social media allow you to hone in on your target audience and speak directly to them. You can bring them valuable products and services, and do it in a way that it is exactly what they need.

They can raise their hands and say, "Hey, I want that!"

That's the way to be in the market, with respect, dignity, and heart. People love when you operate like this, as it sets you apart from your competitors.

When clients came to me, they had invested a lot of money into coaching, mentoring, and a lot of products to *funnel up* their business, as it is called. They were overwhelmed with funnels and sales approaches, and they really hadn't grown their businesses.

Some clients have been taught a lot of marketing methods. Using those methods, they have had to:

» Position themselves
» Go through all the promotion and sales pages
» Try to sell more stuff

...and have to funnel and sell more stuff ...and more stuff

In my business, we were able to forget all of that. We chose not to worry about all the different ways that we could get in front of people and create revenue.

We decided to look at one thing:

What is being talked about on social media?

Take a look at the social media managed by your prospect and ask yourself:

Where is the client's pain?

Where is the client hurting?

What does the client want?

FIND YOUR TARGET AUDIENCE - WITH NO FACEBOOK ADS

Notice we aren't using Facebook ads at all. We are using a totally free strategy to engage qualified prospects and we are serving people and not selling them. We also use Facebook to bring us qualified prospects in a few more ways that cost us absolutely nothing. I am sharing everything and pulling back the curtain in this revised edition!

The other way we use Facebook is to establish a Facebook group that focuses on the keywords that your target audience wants or needs. One of my groups is called Business Owners Marketing and Sales Help (https://www.facebook.com/groups/marketingandsaleshelp).

The name indicates who the group is for as well as the exact outcome I have for the group. As of today, we have, 5,485 members. Every day I post valuable content for discussion and often I do a live broadcast there as well.

When you are the owner of a group, people in the group see you as the expert. I don't pitch there. I create value and give help. When I notice people who are very engaged, I message them and offer a 10-minute game plan session. I also invite people to direct message me if they want more help.

I run about 10 groups like this on Facebook and highly recommend you join this group: https://www.facebook.com/groups/heartrepreneurswithterrilevine I spend most of my time and give the most value here, as this is where my primary focus is.

My final piece of Facebook magic is after setting up a group, creating and running challenges in the group. Let me dig into this because I learned from making a mistake and you can learn from not making the same mistake.

The first time I ran a challenge, (https://www.facebook.com/groups/Terrischallenge) I gave massive value for 5 days and then I did a bonus on day 6 and offered a program that taught more deeply what I had shared.

Because I taught everything, very few people enrolled in the bonus program! When I ran my next challenge, http://facebook.com/groups/10kin45minutes I taught a ton of content and held back a bit about how to actually apply the content easily.

In this case, people had questions and wanted more information. I was able to generate a lot of excited and qualified prospects who then joined my programs because they really wanted more. Lesson learned.

I hope you are getting excited by my Facebook success and seeing some possibilities for your own business. Let me share one client's case study to open you up for even more possibilities!

My client is a very gifted copywriter. He has helped coaches, consultants, speakers, trainers, authors, chiropractors, dentists and even attorneys create great emails, awesome letters, and helped them with web copy and online letters. His business had been super solid, it suddenly took a dip, and he hired me to help him turn his business around fast.

I had him do his Facebook Lives in the group and suggest to his members that they share them. He began his group and initially it was building slowly. I had him do his Facebook Lives in the group and to suggest members share his lives. I also had him share his lives on his personal and business pages when they had been completed.

Within three short weeks his group was close to 250 qualified prospects. Every day, Monday through Friday, he did a Facebook Live, then, for about 20 minutes a day he followed up with direct messages to those people who reached out to him and those people who he felt he wanted to connect with.

He scheduled 17, 10-minute game plan sessions within a month of following my advice. I also shared exactly what to do on those 10-minute calls to create even more value. At the end of conducting those 17 sessions, he had added 9 new copywriting clients and had 4 new clients who enrolled in his do-it-yourself copywriting course. His business had, in fact, turned around. Yes, that quickly!

Our philosophy of giving, giving, giving and serving, serving, serving is what has allowed my clients to command higher prices, as well.

How does this work? Once you know what your prospects really want (not what you think they want) and you can absolutely deliver this to them, you add in more benefits for them.

As an example, in my year-long mentoring program I not only provide weekly mentoring I also bonus my clients by giving them my entire done-for-you marketing library.

The resources in this library cost hundreds of thousands of dollars to build and include market-dominating advertising and marketing ads, customized million-dollar "elevator pitches" (that I refer to as Core Unique Positioning Statements), effective email templates, sales letters, sales scripts, TV ads, secret resources and templates and much, much more.

You can take a peek here: www.theultimatebusinessgrowthsystem.com. By giving away all this content for free along with the mentoring, I increased the price of mentoring by $2,500 and clients are excited to pay this amount to get access to the library along with me.

Here's a client case study to illustrate that commanding higher fees is simple when you add value and give people more of what they do want. This client came to me doing direct sales for a network marketing company. I am a big believer in network marketing and at the same time teach my clients that the brand they represent is themselves and the product or service is what they sell.

This client was a consultant for a very popular health and wellness company. She was making less than $40,000 a year doing direct sales and wanted to make at least $120,000 as she had 2 daughters she was hoping to send to college. I had her become the brand. She became a health and wellness consultant who recommended products that came from this company.

We set up a website and social media presence under her brand name and not the direct sales company. When she sold the products, she would get the same commission, of course, as that is what the company gave every consultant. Most consultants are simply there as agents of the company.

However, she was now more than an agent. She was a health and wellness consultant who helped you, educated you, informed you, and coached you, as well as sharing the products she felt you needed. Within 98 days she had 11 clients each paying her $3000 for a 12-week health and wellness program. That is $33,000 in a little over 3 months! Compare that to her $40,000 for 12 months!

And, it gets better. Product sales happened based on her recommendations and she added $12,000 to her income from those sales. So, in 98 days she earned $47,000! That's more than she earned in the entire year before focusing on adding value and not being afraid to ask for higher fees based on the outcome and value she created!

For literally no money at all—not even for pay-per-click ads or Facebook ads—you can find your target audience. It is possible to see what kind of content the audience truly wants to see.

In my case, after my team found our target audience, we decided to serve them from the highest place we could. We were committed to bringing them not just great practical value—helping them with their problem, showing them how to remove the problem—but also to bring them some unseen perceived value. We brought them intrinsic value, which also helped them in their world.

For example, we created a really fun project with one particular client, a healer. We stopped doing what the client was accustomed to doing, and made them step outside of their comfort zone. Instead, we made a list of all the practical value they brought as a benefit.

We asked:

What do you bring that is a real healing experience, of healing the client's inner child?

How does that help your life?

What does that do for you in your life?

How does that make a difference in your life? Why are people looking for that?

Why are people talking about that on the internet? Why are people hurting so much?

Why do they have so much come up with past patterns, and looking at their old DNA?

We closely examined those issues and wondered how we could help the client solve the problem differently. There were a lot of people out there who were calling themselves shamans, healers, and inner-child workers. We didn't want to be helping only on a practical level—even though the client most definitely could use help on a practical level—we also wanted to be intrinsically different.

To promote the idea that our client had a more valuable service to offer, we raised the fees. When clients see higher fees, they understand that means there's also a higher quality of product. That understanding is the *intrinsic value* of a product or service.

We wanted our client to be the service provider who had higher fees.

This is because consumers understand that someone in the marketplace is going to have higher fees and they will most likely be the one who delivers more.

Many years ago, I changed my coaching rates from $250 a month to $1,500 a month. I did it overnight, and it created a huge waiting list. Two years later I went from $1,500 to $25,000, and I *still* had a huge waiting list.

Charging more works when you show clients that you can:

» Offer more than your competition
» Demonstrate the benefits they will experience
» Do more for your clients

Once my clients showed a greater intrinsic value by increasing their prices, it boosted their profits, increased their customer base, and, their customers started to choose the higher-priced service over the lower.

People tend to be attracted to higher-ticket goods. For example, I think a lot of my clients, even if they owned and loved a Prius, would be really excited if they were offered a Mercedes, BMW, or a Ferrari. They understand those cars cost more money because the market has proven they're worth more—they have a greater intrinsic value.

The whole point here is understanding that not only can you reach more, but—as long as you are truly bringing more—you feel that you have more, you can charge more, and that increases the effectiveness of reaching people, heart to heart, and having them choose you. You have to realize the true worth of the service you are offering (hint, it's probably more than you think).

You can command higher fees and expand your business model when you really deliver benefits for those you serve. In fact, I established a program teaching clients how to create their own signature group programs so that they could work a lot less hours and make a lot more money. I've focused a large part of my business this past year mentoring about 100 people through this process.

I have found that people who invest in higher priced services do so because they are committed to achieving the results these services promise. What does that mean to you? More committed clients. Clients who actually get outcomes. Clients who achieve outcomes become raving fans, are more enjoyable to work with and do what is necessary to achieve the results they say they want.

This is why you want to charge higher fees. Don't just charge higher fees without providing a ton of value. You want to be of high service to your clients and to get them the results they are investing in. Just know that people who invest in higher price services are the target audience to focus on.

Now you have the ability to reach a huge group of your targeted prospects and to gain qualified leads by following the advice in this chapter. As long as you do business heart to heart from a place of honesty, authenticity, transparency, integrity, and produce high value and massive outcomes that your clients really want, you are well on your way to Turbocharging your business!

TREAT CLIENTS WITH RESPECT AND DIGNITY BECAUSE YOU CHOOSE TO

Most businesses are not treating clients as if they are anything more than a number, the next sale or a dollar figure. You can literally steal the clients of other businesses when you make a choice to consider everyone that spends a cent with you as someone who is now a member of your extended family.

What does this really mean? In my life, my family comes first. I think of my family often, I love them, I care for them and about them. I make spontaneous calls to family members. I pick up gifts for them if I see something that they will appreciate or resonate with. My family is always on my mind and in my heart.

My clients come after my family so I consider everyone who has spent any money on my products or services one of my extended family members. I also care for and about them, think of them often, and act the same way towards them as I do with my blood family.

I want you to fall in love with your clients. I want you to embrace them as family and take them under your wing and truly care about them. Business is not just about marketing to people and selling to them. Business is about creating deep heart-centered relationships, allowing people into your client family, and giving them an experience that lets them see that you really do care and they really do matter - always and in all ways.

The internet also offers us a chance to attract other people's clients or prospects and poach them. One of the reasons we have this beautiful, built-in way of having other people's prospects and clients come to us is because most businesses today are so busy hunting for more prospects, more clients, more customers, and more patients, that they're not paying attention to the ones they have. They're not even speaking heart to heart in their marketing; they're very clearly trying to attract somebody by saying,

"Hey, come look at me! Come see me! Come get me!"

When you don't do that, and instead take the opportunity to let people know who you are, and see you putting your heart into it, they instantly feel attracted to you.

Take a look at your competitors. Everyone has competitors- every single one of us. Look at what they're saying. Look at how they're selling. Look at how they're not necessarily in conversations, heart-to-heart and individually, with people.

The very first thing you could do is ask yourself some questions:

How can I show my heart?

How can I position myself differently, not like the big businesses, not exerting effort to attract people, and not pressuring them to come on board?

Can we be more magnetic by allowing our prospects and customers to see that they matter to us, and that we want them to be significant when they come to buy our products and services?

Nowadays, a lot of people have taught marketing in a style that demonstrates a problem and then shows how we're the solution. Being a Heart-repreneur®, one of the best ways that you can attract people magnetically is *not* to do that, absolutely *not* do that, but instead go against what everybody teaches.

Just stay visible.

Give messages like:

» "Look, I care."
» "You matter."
» "I have some solutions and I'm going to let you in on them."
» "I'm not going to agitate your problem; I'm here to help you with your problem."
» "I get you. I feel you. I understand you, and I choose to serve you." Be contrary to the way most people are doing business today.

RISE TO THE TOP AND STAY THERE

When you stand out from your competitors by delivering outcomes, truly caring about clients and treating clients like family, you will rise to the top in your niche.

The people who serve their niche from the place of the highest good, creates real value for their clients, comes from a place of serving, rises to the top in their field and becomes known as the go-to authority.

They are considered a celebrity in their field. These people have qualified prospects who are constantly attracted to them. Once you reach this pinnacle, by following the path I have laid out, your business will soar to the top. Achieving celebrity status is the result of being seen as the credible expert in your area of specialty.

You don't go claim this by saying you are an expert or authority or guru. Think about celebrity actors and musicians. They don't say, "I'm a Rockstar" or "I'm the jazz expert". We label them once we see them and position them this way. Give your clients and prospects what they want and need, over deliver, wow them, and they will create celebrity status for you.

Let's deep dive into this concept.

To get noticed in today's marketplace, you have to have a position in the marketplace and continue to hold it. Some businesses don't hold a position because they're generalists; they're speaking to everyone.

When you move up the ladder, you may look at how people get positioned.

Some people will say, "Oh, I won't be a generalist. I'll be very niched. I'll be a specialist, and I'll be known for a specialty."

The marketplace has really promoted that. There are *authorities* in our field, the number one, the best one. If you're going to hire a business consultant, you need to hire the authority of business consulting. If you're going to hire a financial planner, you want that authority.

There's something even greater than that. This is where somebody really has risen to the pinnacle, and is attracting the majority of the business.

I call this person a *celebrity*.

I call them a celebrity because they're going to be noticed in the marketplace, the marketplace is going to get excited about them, and it's going to choose them.

Their position is going to mimic exactly the celebrities that we watch on television, in movies, or in print. There's a real attraction to famous people. Being positioned as a celebrity will take your business right to the top of the charts.

In the first edition of *Turbocharge,* I talked about taking a stand to also set yourself apart. I still believe you need to speak up for what you believe even if it isn't popular and may be controversial. I am not talking about sex, religion or politics! I am saying to take a stand in your niche and be vocal on and off-line about what you believe.

Advocate for what you and your business stand for. Clients do business with companies and people who speak out and take stands for what they believe in. In fact, like-minded prospects will show up who agree with you. You will create an emotional connection with your audience and they will become interested in your services and products.

BECOME THE CELEBRITY IN YOUR FIELD WITH EASE

Who is your favorite celebrity? What singer, musician, actor or mentor do you admire most?

That person got to hold that celebrity position because they got known for some specific skill or talent. They started out doing what they do without being known for their gifts. They delivered something people saw as awesome, then those people saw them as unique and special, became their raving fans, encouraged more people to experience them, soon, they had a following of fans and boom - celebrity status was given to them.

Is there a celebrity in your niche?

Today I was speaking with a client who is a personal trainer. I asked him this same question. He said Jillian Michaels was the celebrity trainer. I asked him what it might take to be a celebrity like Jillian. He told me he would need a TV show.

I suggested he begin with any of these ideas - write a book, create a YouTube TV channel, start some Facebook groups and communities, host some live events and fitness challenges, give away free tips on

CHAPTER ONE - THE EXPANDED HEART-REPRENEUR® PHILOSOPHY

personal training, write some articles, start blogging, host a podcast, do some webinars, be active on Facebook Live, and get interviewed on TV and radio.

Just putting no more than 2 or 3 of these ideas in place will propel him to the top of his niche so he can become a celebrity like Jillian. This is exactly how my clients from app developers to business consultants to dog groomers to educators to residential cleaners and veterinarians and physicians and attorneys and on and on, have become celebrities in their niches.

When I entered the field of coaching, Tony Robbins was the big celebrity in my field. I wanted to be known as the top business coach and consultant the way he had become known as the leading life coach. I imitated the actions he took to gain celebrity status and modified them to better fit my personality.

You don't need to spend a lot of money to position yourself as a celebrity. You don't even need to invest money on branding. By using the internet wisely and correctly, you can soon be perceived as a celebrity in your field.

I told you in the first edition of *Turbocharge* that you can position yourself, your expertise and your gifts through your presence on the internet. When you understand your target audience, who they are, how they think, the results they desire, you relate to them heart to heart, fulfill their needs on social media, interact with them and are of service to them, the celebrity positioning becomes automatic.

Begin to see yourself as the true expert in your niche. Act as if you already are by creating an impact on others. Soon, your target audience will follow your lead and you will be perceived as a celebrity.

Do you want to spend your valuable time hunting for qualified leads? Or would you rather spend your time with your family, on vacations, serving your paid client family and living your life fully having money rolling in and freedom rolling out? If you are like my clients, and I assume you are, you would prefer qualified leads coming to you, raising their hands and showing interest in the services you provide.

Yes?

Decide right in this moment what niche you choose to be a celebrity in. Start to create value every single day for people in that niche.

Here's a case study of exactly how I did this for a client.

When this client came to me she was a profitability coach. She wanted to be seen as the celebrity who could help any dental practice double their profits. The "fame plan" I set up for her had her hosting a podcast and interviewing dentists on her show, teaching profit tips to dentists on an automated webinar and writing a short print book on this topic and giving this book away all over the internet for the cost of shipping only.

Within 96 days she had 1,000 dentists who were now connected to her. She created value for those thousand dentists through podcasts, tip sheets, and webinars. I told her to begin seeing herself as the celebrity in the niche of helping dentists become more profitable.

We even worked on a few visioning techniques so that she could really feel herself, see herself, and begin to believe she was the go-to person for dentists who wanted more profitable practices. This relates to a concept that I addressed in the first edition of this book. Whatever we focus on is exactly what we end up getting. Whatever we believe is exactly what we achieve.

Every day she spent a few minutes reading her vision statement and putting herself in the mindset of being that celebrity person and she began to act as if she already was. What I mean by act as if, is she began to speak with more authority and conviction to use the words that conveyed the fact that she was an expert in her field without saying I am the "expert".

You can also be positioned as the celebrity and the expert in your field. If you truly want to impact people, make a difference and be of service, then it is important that you share what you do with as many people as possible in order to become the sought-after expert.

CHAPTER ONE - THE EXPANDED HEART-REPRENEUR® PHILOSOPHY

This is not a case of being famous because your ego wants you to be famous. You want to be well known so that people can find you more easily, access your services so you can bring your gift to the world, bring your solutions to those who serve others and truly help those that you serve.

If you recall, in the first edition of *Turbocharge* I talked about your Core Unique Positioning Statement. This is the statement that helps you gain status as the go-to expert in your field. This one statement tells how you achieve the results that you achieve and actually are different than any other person in your niche.

When I help my clients formulate a statement like this I typically have them start by saying I am "the only". The words "the only" instantly position you as the one person or the one company that can truly help clients get what it is they desire and deserve. You cannot just say that you are "the only" if in fact other people can do or deliver exactly what it is that you do or provide. You must think about how you are different.

It might be your background, it might be your experience, it might be the system that you use or the method that you have developed or created, it might be the way you serve people, it might be your guaranteed outcome or result.

Once you have created a statement that represents how you are different and positions you in this way you must begin to use that statement everywhere. It should be on your business cards, on your social media profiles, in your signature files, in your email, on your letterhead, on your website, in your byline, and what you say when introducing yourself at networking events.

You get to control how your audience sees you. However you want to be perceived is how you must position yourself. If you want people to see you as different and unique and as the celebrity in your field, who they really want to do business with, then you want to spend some time creating a great Core Unique Positioning Statement that will instantly attract people to you.

If you were my client, I would ask you to name your favorite celebrity, or somebody you admire.

We'd look at that person. Then I'd ask you to look at the celebrity's positioning.

How did they get positioned as a celebrity? There are some people who are paid hundreds of thousands of dollars for a short speech.

How did they get there?

They might not be the best speakers. There may be other phenomenal speakers available, but the celebrity did something to position themselves. If we can look at someone like that, we can learn how to imitate that celebrity.

Examine your marketplace. There's nobody more magnetic to customers in the marketplace than someone who's a celebrity.

Who is a celebrity in your marketplace?

As I mentioned before, when I entered the field of coaching, Tony Robbins was the big celebrity in my field.

I thought: *How did he get to be who he is?*

I read a lot about him, and I recommend you do the same. I studied him; he was just like anybody else. He was struggling to make a living, and then he had this idea of doing infomercials. The infomercials positioned him; they made him who he is.

Ask yourself: *How can I position myself so that the marketplace has an image of me and sees me at the top?*

Positioning for a Heart-repreneur® is different than for a large corporation that spends hundreds of thousands of dollars on branding and positioning. The great news is, we as individuals don't need to. The internet gives us the opportunity to position ourselves as the celebrity.

You can use the internet to introduce yourself to people. Then you can guide the marketplace to think whatever it is you want them to think about you, as long as it's authentic and honest. You need to identify the kind of character that your marketplace wants.

- » Be the person that your marketplace is looking for.
- » Be the business that it's looking for.
- » Define what the market perceives as having high intrinsic value, and be that.

Once you take that stance, you will magnetize your ideal clients, your ideal prospects, and build a heart-based business all at once.

PROMOTION AND POSITIONING—NOT MARKETING AND SELLING

Once we have your Core Unique Positioning and we know exactly what it is, we have to deploy it.

This can be challenging because of a couple of different reasons.

There are two common ways that people can miss opportunities:

1. **People don't differentiate themselves from competition well enough.** Often, I look at websites and see that they look similar. For example, I work with a lot of dentists. I've looked at thousands of their sites. The sites are designed by the same web companies. They all have the same words, and the same stock images, but there's not a Core Unique Positioning in the individual sites.

2. **There isn't good promotion.** In the cases where somebody *has* come up with a good Core Unique Positioning Statement, or a great brand, but still experience marketing trouble, I find the same thing; they do not have a good promotional strategy. So even though the business has claimed its position, it hasn't deployed it and promoted it. Without promotion, you're not going to go very far. You're going to have a position, but the position's not going to be known by anyone, so it won't do anything.

One of my mentors has a concept called *pre-framing*, in which you effect and impact people even before they buy your product or service. When you pre-frame, you reach your prospects in any number of ways.

They may:

- » Read something about you or by you
- » Hear you on the radio or a podcast
- » See you at an event or in a YouTube video
- » Visit your website or your social media page

Psychologically, they will already see you as a big celebrity in the field because you're visible. You're taking a stand.

When you create a presence by pre-framing, you're not pitching to people at all. You're sharing a message with them that's true and from your heart.

I love this concept, and I think it's important to follow even before you start promoting. Again, most businesses do not do this.

You should make sure you've pre-framed that celebrity piece before anyone:

- » Interacts with you
- » Reads your blog post
- » Introduces you on-stage
- » Walks into your store
- » Goes to your website
- » Looks at anything related to your business

You want to make sure that people have seen you and realize:

This is a celebrity.

You can do that, very simply, by using the internet. Once again, when we take advantage of the internet, we're reaching millions and millions of people for little or no cost.

How can you do this?

- » Make some simple videos and upload them to YouTube.
- » Syndicate some articles or blog posts.
- » Comment on forums.
- » Make contributions on sites like www.selfgrowth.com.

Put yourself out there and make sure that you are not only positioned, but you also put your stake in the ground. You promote yourself in the marketplace *without* marketing.

Declare: "Here's what I do that makes me super. Here's what makes me the one to work with in this niche. Here's what I stand against in the niche, and what I stand for."

When I first started coaching, I was in a crowd of about 25,000 other coaches.

I asked myself: *How am I going to be different?*

I took a real serious stand within the coaching industry. While I carried the credentials of Master Certified Coach—which is the highest level that you can attain in a coaching profession—I recognized that the rank was not what brought me major clients like General Electric. They didn't care about that.

What set me apart is that I took a stand in the coaching industry about something I really believed in. My clients did *not* come to me because of having made-up coaching credentials within the coaching industry.

Because I had quickly built a very successful business while most coaches were struggling, I positioned myself as an authority on how to get clients for coaches. Then I embraced the position and promoted myself as a celebrity. I came out loudly staking my claim in the marketplace, saying what I was for and what I was against.

I wasn't afraid to take that stand because I believed wholeheartedly in that position. Pretty soon, I was a celebrity in my field. I was dubbed by the press, "The Guru of Coaching."® I did all this using pre-framing, though I didn't realize it at the time and hadn't had a name for it yet.

FOCUS ON POSITIONING—NOT MARKETING AND SELLING

I'm going to go beyond the conversation that we had in the first edition of *Turbocharge*. In the first addition, I talk a bit about how to deploy your Core Unique Positioning Statement and why this is sometimes a bit challenging for people.

Since the book was published I have probably worked with another thousand or more people and really have assisted people to create their Core Unique Positioning Statements in an easy and effortless way that allows them to be properly positioned without having to use expensive marketing techniques or sales methods.

The first step in positioning yourself as unique is to pick a word that goes with "the only" that describes the outcome you deliver. As an example, in my business my words are: I am the only business strategist ... I define who I am right away.

Next, pick an action verb that tells what you do. The following examples come from the clients who I have created Core Unique Positioning Statements for:

» Support
» Help
» Guide
» Mentor
» Teach
» Serve
» Provide
» Assist
» Aid

» Give

» Evaluate

» Assess

In my case it is I am the only business strategist who helps...

Now I want you to stir up what is really bugging your qualified leads to want to get rid of their problem or what is driving them to leave the pain and meet their goals.

Client examples include:

» Stressed

» Frustrated

» Anxious

» Overwhelmed

» Upset

» Scared

» Desperate

» Uncertain

» Angry

» Concerned

» Ill

In my business, it is stated in this way - I am the only business strategist who helps frustrated, struggling ...

Now it is time to tell exactly and specifically who you help so your target audience can decide if what you have is for them and if they are a fit for your services or products.

» Client examples include:

» Overweight moms

» Teenagers

» Cat lovers

- Chronic pain sufferers
- Homeowners
- Business owners
- Brides-to-Be
- New moms

Adding to my own Core Unique Positioning Statement I define my clients by saying, "I am the only business strategist who helps frustrated, struggling service providers of heart-based businesses ..."

Next, you want to use the words that prospects and clients gave you when you did the research asking them the one result they wanted from you. Here are some words my clients shared when doing this coaching assignment:

- Increase profits
- Purchase the perfect home
- Get the pain relief I need
- Find a doctor who really listens
- Get a therapist who really understands me
- Help me start a successful business
- Get the weight off once and for all
- Help me get back into my smaller size clothes
- Generate qualified leads
- Make more money

My Core Unique Positioning Statement with that addition is, "I am the only business strategist who helps frustrated, struggling service providers of heart-based businesses with my proprietary, simple 3-step method called Command, Connect, Covert. This process helps you command more qualified leads fast, to connect with those leads heart to heart with ease and joy and to convert those leads into high paying clients without selling - guaranteed."

Notice that the complete Core Unique Positioning Statement tells my solution, gives my process a proprietary method, lets my prospects know it is simple and has a guarantee built in. Also note I am providing the benefits that I uncovered during my research.

My prospects and clients told me they wanted more leads and they wanted them fast, they wanted a way to enjoy connecting with those qualified leads and they wanted to offer high ticket programs and services and did not want to use sales tactics. I am giving them what they want through my business mentoring programs and I also add a guarantee. The process, the results, and the guarantee combine to make me "the only".

The benefits of the outcome and results I deliver "Command Connect Convert" are built right into my Core Unique Positioning Statement as well.

Once you create this statement you must use it everywhere. I found out that after people read *Turbocharge* they began to craft these statements and then they weren't sure how to tweak them to use them when speaking, when networking and in offline and online copy, so let me give you some examples to help you further.

The biggest reason to become a celebrity is that as soon as you have positioned yourself as such, you become sought-after. You become known as something or someone special. People are very attracted to those they perceive as celebrities.

We're a society that's very star struck, and very interested in who's at the top.

Ask yourself:

Who is my target audience?

What will I be famous for?

How am I different from other people?

In one particular case, for example, my client wasn't famous at all, but we stated that the client was. We actually used the word "famous." We stated that the client is famous for helping people who are struggling in their business to get loans even though they might not qualify for them.

That's how you position and advertise yourself as a celebrity. It's a good way to position yourself in the marketplace.

Use some positioning words. One of the words I just shared with you is "famous." When you refer to yourself as famous, people will follow suit. Although you may think to yourself, *Well, I'm not really famous yet*, you must take a stance and you must believe—you must truly feel and resonate with the idea that you are famous.

We get what we focus on.

If we can imagine that we're standing in front of millions and millions of people with our message, with our product, with our service, and we really believe in our product or service, then our desired position takes on greater importance.

Our position must be important because in order to share our mission with thousands, or hundreds of thousands, or even millions, we must claim the celebrity stake. We must own it. If your mission is important enough, you'll feel good about saying that you are sought-after, that you are the expert, that you are famous.

What you put out there is what you will attract. You must:

» Put yourself out there
» Claim what I call your Core Unique Positioning Statement
» Come up with something that makes you different
» Become the expert
» Position yourself above everybody else

Then it's important that you integrate that message into everything you do.

Everything that communicates your brand—*everything*—must reflect that same desired perception. This includes:

- Social media
- Signature files
- Anything written
- Anything spoken
- Your product line in stores or on websites

Everything must reflect that same desired perception. You want people to perceive you as a celebrity before your audience has ever done business with you.

It's important that you are positioned correctly and that you keep the positioning in an integrated way.

You want people to be able to:

- Hear you
- See you
- Know about you

People will see you and instantly recognize, "This is the leader, the expert celebrity in that field."

WHY BEING A CELEBRITY MATTERS

Let's say I needed to stand up at a networking meeting and give a 30 second commercial or elevator pitch. This is how I would take my Core Unique Positioning Statement and make it work there.

A reminder - here is the statement: "I am the only business strategist who helps frustrated, struggling service providers of heart-based businesses with my proprietary simple 3 step method called Command, Connect, Covert. This process helps you command more qualified leads fast, to connect with those leads heart to heart with ease and joy and to convert those leads into high paying clients without selling - guaranteed."

30 second commercial:

"Do you know how business owners today are desperately seeking proven solutions to help them grow their business? My company has created *The Ultimate Business Growth System* that gives small business owners and entrepreneurs who love doing business with heart, a proprietary system to command all the qualified leads they want, a way to connect with those leads heart to heart and a process to convert those qualified leads into clients without selling them, and the system is guaranteed."

Your Core Unique Positioning Statement is a message that is created in truth and with authenticity and transparency and must have the integrity of what you realistically can deliver for clients.

The more passionate you are about helping people, sharing this message and making a difference in the lives and businesses of those you serve, the more this message will be heard as heartfelt and will land the people who are qualified to work with you.

By having a well-crafted Core Unique Positioning Statement, you will position yourself as a trusted expert and be well on your way to creating celebrity status in your specific market. You don't have to walk around calling yourself "America's leading expert" or "Guru of XYZ".

Your statement begins to clearly show people you are unique, you are different and you should be noticed. Of course, you must deliver the results you say you can obtain for clients or your celebrity status will fade away fast.

Now that you have this statement I want you to put it everywhere. I want you to be very conscious of saying it and using it and placing it on the Internet as well as in print. Then let's get on to having even more people find out about you.

In addition to the Facebook group strategy and Facebook Live strategy I shared earlier, I have one more strategy that is my secret sauce that will help qualified prospects find you and will place you into the dominant position in your niche.

Millions and millions of people watch YouTube videos. YouTube only began on February 14, 2005 and it ranks as the 3rd most visited website in the world. Ready for this? The total number of people who use YouTube is 1,300,000,000 and 300 hours of video are uploaded to YouTube every minute!

In fact, almost 5 billion videos are watched on YouTube every day with over 30 million visitors per day. Wait! There's more! In a survey 6 out of 10 people preferred online video platforms to live TV and the number of hours people spend watching videos on YouTube is up 60% year after year. Have I convinced you that YouTube is important? I sure hope so.

So, what can you do with YouTube to create massive credibility and celebrity status? Let me share some ideas that I have coached my clients to use.

Create a lot of training, teaching and educational content that your ideal target audience would be interested in that will help them avoid pain or to reach their goals. By starting your own YouTube channel and posting video content there you will develop a fan base interested in your material and in your services.

You can make these short videos, even one minute long. How-to videos are super popular on YouTube so keep this in mind when deciding what content to post. The goal of your YouTube channel is to create followers who have a keen interest in your videos.

Be certain your videos aren't done to sell anything. They should show your expertise and your passion so that people want to follow you.

Use the YouTube Dashboard to see which of your followers interact with your channel the most, then reach out to them, thank them, and open up some dialogue with them. They are your best prospects.

Be sure your videos end with a call to action like, "subscribe to my channel" or "watch my next video". It is important that you prompt people to subscribe to your channel. This is how you will grow your channel and your influence.

Inform your followers on all your other social media platforms about your YouTube channel and suggest videos to them.

Make your videos fun and entertaining. People won't stay very long if the videos are a boring talking head. Make your video like a fun TV commercial.

Slow and steady wins the race. Growing your YouTube channel takes time and patience. It is worth the effort.

I put up 100 YouTube videos a few years ago on my channel (https://www.youtube.com/user/coachterri) teaching things prospects and clients wanted to learn. Each video is about one minute in length and I received a lot of prospects from this.

I am just now starting a TV show that will soon be seen on YouTube called TerriTV (www.Terri.TV) and I believe that will also require some patience and creativity to grow my audience. I am doing this because I have seen that YouTubers create loyal audiences and qualified leads. (That's a hint!)

Are you seeing how to get known without a lot of hype with no expense?

Remember, your Core Unique Positioning Statement is the basis of all your marketing and positioning. It should be obvious from what people see online and offline that you are different.

Over $10,000 in bonus free courses, programs and trainings are available to you as a reader when you create a free account here: https://www.heartrepreneuracademy.com/

CREATE YOUR MAGNET: DEVELOP AN AFFINITY

Many people in business pick the niche, product, or service without having a true affinity for the market.

Maybe you're tempted to pick that niche because you think: *I'll get into internet marketing* (or IT consulting, or whatever) *because there's a lot of money to be made there.*

It may be true that there's money to be made, but without that heart connection, people can't resonate with you. If they don't get a feel for how you are connected to their market, they can't really believe in you. It's very difficult to attract customers.

For example, I work with a lot of dentists.

People might ask, "Well, Terri, what does your work have to do with dentists?"

They might wonder how I have any connection with the dental marketplace when I'm not a dentist and have never worked in the dental profession.

I created an affinity.

I wrote newsletters and articles; I volunteered columns for magazines. I interviewed dentists on my radio show, made sure they were the focus. I read everything I could about dentists.

I wanted to know:

What were they attracted to? What were they not attracted to?

What kinds of people did they want to hire? Who didn't they want to hire?

I looked at dental websites. I looked at every single thing I could get my hands on related to dentists. I joined associations that accepted non-dentist members. I even made friends with some very high-level dentists who went to dental meetings, and brought me along as their friend.

Up until that point the only dentist I knew was my own family dentist, who had no interest in my business or working with me.

To develop an affinity, all I did was put a message out to the market that said, "Look, I'm concerned about dentists and their issues."

The message came from my actions: I interviewed dentists and based on what I found, I applied my areas of expertise and skill to help that particular market.

I didn't do it looking for the market to reward me; I did it to help the market. I did whatever I could do to help people in the dental business.

You want to make sure as you're creating an affinity with a market, that you are truly understanding your market. If you find that you're in a market that you don't care a lot about, *get out*. Get into a market where you really want to do business with the people there—where you can really care about the people, their issues, and their problems.

» Take the time, the energy, and the money to get into their market.
» Understand their market.
» Know everything you can about the market.
» Put yourself in relation with the market, so that you're part of the market.

At this point, even though I'm a business mentor, not a dentist, I'm invited to the same dental seminars, conferences, and study groups, and invited to write for dental magazines and websites. That is because I created an affinity with the specific marketplace.

In my experience with my clients, their income directly relates to how well they have established goodwill and affinity in the marketplace.

The more you establish and maintain goodwill in the marketplace and the more you really care about the marketplace, the more your goods and services will be the obvious choice for that marketplace.

There are two very common ways that you might get this wrong:

1. **You really don't care about a particular market.** You just don't. You're marketing to a market because you think that there's money there, or you think it's easy, or whatever it might be.
2. **The market can tell that, and they don't trust you.** When they don't trust you, they're not going to be drawn to purchase from you.

So, remember, you want to build a lot of intrinsic value, and you want to show people that you really care about their niche, and that's why you're in that niche.

USE STRATEGIC ALLIANCES TO GET KNOWN FAST

I want you to build your business really fast. After all the name of this book IS *Turbocharge Your Business*! As a business strategist, I speak with business owners from all over the world almost every day.

The common problems I hear are: These very heart-centered business owners are struggling to command high quality leads. They don't know how to deeply connect with the leads they do have to build relationships with them. Then, they aren't able to convert leads into clients because they don't like to sell and don't know how to get people to say "yes".

Is any of this resonating with you?

I have great news for you! You can use strategic alliances to grow your business and to also get known as an expert really quickly. I love sharing this strategy with my clients because it has no upfront costs and results in clients and income.

Think of a strategic alliance as two or more businesses forming a relationship to share markets or to endorse a product or service to their own client base and then exchanging a portion of the revenue from the sales made from the alliance.

Before rushing into strategic alliances, I want you to hit the pause button and ask yourself two really important questions:

First, who is your exact target audience and what characteristics do your ideal prospects and clients possess?

Second, who else do your ideal clients do business with before or after they engage in your services?

Here is one of my clients as an example.

This client is a life coach helping people decrease stress and increase peace in their lives. She is seeking women ages 25-55 who are very tired, overwhelmed in life and at work and want to enjoy their lives and their work more.

She decided that massage therapists, spas, fitness centers, gyms, wellness centers, yoga studios, and chiropractors were good strategic alliance partners.

I had her create a big list of all the possible partners in her geographic area. The people she did know in the area are the first people I had her approach. The approach was effortless and was nothing more than calling these people and explaining her alliance concept and sharing how it would benefit both businesses.

She focused on how the agreement would be of service to the alliance partner and to their clients.

Because she wanted her alliance partners to know her services and really trust their clients would get value from using her services, she offered each partner a session with her so they could try her on and get comfortable with her skills and the value she could provide their clients.

If you come at this really wanting to serve your alliance partners, to make a difference for their business, their clients, can come up with ways to get them increased exposure, greater credibility, and celebrity status, then saying yes to your alliance offer becomes a no-brainer for them.

One strategy I developed for a client was to bundle their services with their partner. Their partner had a non-competing hypnosis product and my client had a stop-smoking product. These two products were bundled as they complemented each other and each provided benefits to the other's clients. We created a separate offering for their clients, which provided exceptional value.

When you make heart-to-heart connections to serve the highest good of your prospects and the clients of those who you want to enter an alliance with it is truly a win-win-win! It is great business and grows your business very fast.

Reach out to those who you want to create an alliance with and watch both of your businesses expand, grow and see how quickly you can become a leading expert in your niche. Just be certain to come from a heart-centered place of helping the other business owner and creating a lot of value for their clients.

Don't be attached to the outcome of growing your business and making money. I find that whenever I focus on helping someone else expand their business and serve more people, I get just what I need as well.

Remember what Zig Ziglar said? This is how I live in my business and my life. My personal quote that I modified over the years based on the original Ziglar quote is, "Focus on serving, helping, and doing good in the world. You will find everything you give comes back to you multiplied - it's universal law".

MONKEY MIND YOU NO LONGER CONTROL ME - I'M IN CHARGE NOW!

What is on your mind right now as you are reading this book? Are you thinking about all the things you need to get done at home or at work? Are you worried or stressed about something? Are you thinking about the future or the past instead of living in the moment for the moment?

The human brain has about 50,000-70,000 thoughts per day, this means between 35 and 48 thoughts per minute per person! No wonder you feel tired or stressed or confused or worried. That's a lot to keep track of.

Buddha talked about our brains as if they are filled with monkeys jumping from branch to branch while they scream and chatter. Picture the branches each filled with a monkey of your thoughts and emotions trying to get all your attention and wanting to be louder than the other monkeys so it will get noticed.

Then think of the monkey that is filled with fear who tries to take over all the other monkeys and to occupy your brain full-time telling you everything that might go wrong. These monkeys are all swinging from

CHAPTER ONE - THE EXPANDED HEART-REPRENEUR® PHILOSOPHY

branch to branch and your mind is going from one thought to another with thoughts rushing in and rushing out.

It's overwhelming, right? All this activity causes stress, anger, upset, worry, and maybe even sleepless nights. At times, you might think your mind has gone out of control.

I understand the feelings the monkey mind chattering away can cause. About 21 years ago my mind chatter was so loud that I rarely had a sense of calm and longed-for peace and tranquility. I learned a process that has made a dramatic difference for me that I now teach to all the business owners who allow me to embrace and nurture them and take them under my wing. The process is called GID.

Before I introduce you to this process that has quieted my monkey mind and added to my ability to live a blissful and delicious life, let me tell you that just becoming aware of your mind and understanding how your mind is like monkeys fighting for attention, you have already brought this to your consciousness which means you are ahead of most human beings on the planet.

How can you possibly have a very successful business if your mind is screeching at you with so many competing messages? How can you be clear and focused on your work, your clients and achieving outcomes if you are receiving stimuli that is overloading you? If you are not living in the moment then you are missing the precious juice of life.

What I want for you is to have the ability to quiet your mind so that you can be calm and focused and have day to day peace to enjoy your business and your life while being fully present with each and every experience. You deserve this and so do the clients you will be serving as a Heart-repreneur®.

Ok, here is the GID process. Let me just say that I have about 32 unsolicited testimonials from clients I have introduced this process to saying how much it calmed them and allowed them more focus and creativity in their work and that they received a lot of new clients once their brains had cleared this space! Exciting, yes?

G: Gratitude. Every day before your feet hit the floor write down in a journal the things you are grateful for. No matter how small. For example, my journal from today has: living at the beach, my amazing clients, the webinar I am doing tonight, seeing my husband tomorrow, the fresh clean foods I am eating, my new workout regimen, my friends, the comfy shoes I get to wear, all my technology that supports me with the work I do, my health, my creativity, my energy, my ability to give and receive love.

I: Intentions. When my mother left her physical body in 1996 and my friend, Marni, died one week after, at the age of 40, of breast cancer, I woke up. I began to live my life with intention and purpose and started intentionally creating my experiences and making choices that were aligned with my purpose.

I threw away my day planner that I had carried for almost 20 years and had thought I could not live without - it was like my bible at the time. I decided I didn't want to be known for all the things I could do or could get done and that life was more than a daily to-do list. The only time I would be done with my to-dos is when I was to-done - which meant, in the grave.

Instead, each day I wake up and set 3 (no more than 3) intentions for how I want to feel during that day. Then I take inspired actions all day from those intentions. Prior to doing this I used to write down things like "drop off the dry cleaning". Seriously? Is that the most important focus for my life? NO! I want you to write down no more than 3 intentions for how you are choosing to experience your day each and every day prior to getting out of bed.

Put them in your phone or carry them around on an index card. Then, as the day goes on be certain you are focused on those intentions and only take actions aligned with them. Yesterday my intentions were: have fun, deeply connect, and create value. I took actions all day that oscillated with those frequencies.

D: Delegations. There are a lot of things I simply can't figure out and am not sure how they are going to happen. I recall a few years ago wanting to quickly raise $88,000 for my foundation (http://terrilevinefoundationforchildrenwithrsd.org/).

I had no idea how I was going to get that amount of money in for a child who needed treatment urgently. I delegated it to the Universe (you can say God, Spirit, or whatever works for you). I trusted some higher power to guide me and figure this out.

A few days later I was mentoring a business owner who mentioned he also has a company that helps non-profits raise funds. I told him about this girl who really needed our help and to get the treatment she needed that was scheduled 2 weeks out, my foundation needed to raise $88,000. He told me he had the solution and he actually did!

That's how the universe works when I delegate, give up, and give over to it producing solutions for me. Every day think about what is causing your mind to be in fear or stress or problem-solving mode and give all of that over to the universe. As I do this process I always breathe deeply and smile at the same time and trust what I need is being handled. And so, it is!

When your monkey mind chatters at you during the day just tell it to shut the fuc* up, take a nice deep breath and as you breathe, smile. This will stop your anxious thoughts and calm them. Then get yourself into the moment and let go of the past and the future. Live in the moment for the moment and enjoy it.

We can't be certain of other moments, can we? You know your birthdate, yet you don't know your checkout date, so be still, enjoy, and find the good in this moment. Ask yourself, "What is going well and going right in this moment?" and fully allow yourself to answer that question for at least 17 seconds. Why 17 seconds? Quantum physics says like energy attracts more like energy and 17 seconds is what it takes to have this momentum of energy.

The more positive thoughts you have about what is going right the more of those experiences you will create. Research shows that repeated thoughts create neural pathways. The more you focus on the positive aspects of your life, the more permanent those pathways become.

In addition, your daily practice of GID will train your brain to find the positive, since you will be coming from an attitude of gratitude. This will keep those monkeys quiet.

The mind is the biggest obstacle for many people. It stops them from being incredibly successful and making the kind of money that they strive to make.

Your mind and your thoughts can get in the way. Some of the most talented people I've met are struggling. They never get the high profits that they want.

It has nothing to do with their products, their services, or their skills. They might have the most amazing business on the planet.

The issue that I see most often is that people stop themselves. They think negative thoughts like:

I can't have this.

I'm not deserving.

This is going to be hard.

I'm going to have to struggle.

The solution is to get the brain—the mind—in alignment before you go into the marketplace. You've got to make sure that your mind is quiet.

BUILDING FOCUS AND CLARITY

Each day you have your 3 intentions. As you do your work, keep your intentions in mind. Keep on task, keep your productivity and focus by not allowing yourself to get distracted.

If you surround yourself with things that will not distract you and a clear environment you will be able to get more done. Make sure your office space has only what you need available to work on in that moment.

Right now, my desk has only my working notes for this book and nothing else. My cell phone is turned off, as is my email and all social media notifications. I am focused on the intention of writing this book from a place of connection and with love.

One of my clients refers to her lack of focus as "squirrel syndrome". See if you can relate. She says that while she is working on something her brain thinks of something else and she stops what she is working on to begin something else. She also tells me she gets interrupted by calls and emails and heads to social media where she is buried for 30 minutes or more each time.

Another one of my clients has reported that he has so many ideas he is "all over the place" and doesn't know what he should be doing.

Can you relate at all? My guess is you can. I've mentored over 5,000 business owners during the past decades and this is a pattern that we entrepreneurs have. We have a lot of ideas and thoughts and we tend to distract ourselves with shiny objects.

I give my clients these solutions:

Write down all ideas that come to you on index cards. Then file them in a box that is your idea box that sits on your desk or jot them in notes in your phone. When you have completed the project you are working on, then you can look through your ideas and pick ONE to work on from the file of ideas.

This way you never lose the ideas and don't have to keep them in your head or run to them right now fearing you will later forget the idea.

Use a timer and work on your business for 45-55 minutes at a time. Get focused and don't multi-task. When the timer goes off clear your mind. Call a friend, drink some water, take a walk, play a game, whatever relaxes you and will make you happy in that moment.

You will get a lot done with this focused, productive way of working, will enjoy your days a lot more, and most likely will also find you are more creative when you use this process.

YOUR THOUGHTS DETERMINE YOUR SUCCESS

Napoleon Hill, author of *Think and Grow Rich*, said, "Whatever the mind can conceive and believe, the mind can achieve." I totally agree with this and have found this to be true. Whatever it is that you think about the most is what will show up in your business and your life.

If you are thinking about how difficult business is or how few qualified leads you have or the lack of money in your bank account then you will attract more of the things you do not want into your business and your life.

Let me share this client story to illustrate how the mind works in stopping people from obtaining the business success they desire.

One day I was doing a strategy session with a qualified prospect who I was excited to help. I wanted to learn about her business and give her some tips, tools and strategies for success. She owned a hair salon and did some network marketing.

She kept telling me the things she didn't want to have and didn't want to have happen. After she spoke for about 12 minutes I reflected back to her all the things she was talking about and explained to her she wasn't pushing them away by talking about them.

I shared with her that the more she thought of them or spoke about them the more she was going to attract. The Law of Attraction says that like attracts like and she was ordering up more of what she didn't want!

I helped her during the strategy session to see that her own thoughts were creating her feelings and those feelings were bringing the experiences directly to her. I got her talking about things she enjoyed in her business like her clients and focused on her gratitude and passion and shifted her to feeling more joy and more love.

A lot of business and marketing strategists work only on actions to take. I believe that without working on mindset first, a client is not set up for success. Their self-talk will get in their way every single time unless you take the time to guide them to habitually think thoughts that will support the outcomes they desire in their business and in their life. Life coaching must come into play when you are dealing with someone's business because they are a human being living a life who just happens to be building a business.

This prospect became a client, she does the GID process each day, is very aware of her thoughts and also what she is speaking out loud now. She reported to me that she is having great days and meeting more like-minded people in the two short weeks since we started together. She told me she is in a great mood most of the time and her assistant commented to her that she is always whistling.

Last week she attended a networking meeting and met 3 people who are ideal clients for her business and believes 2 of them will be doing business with her now and the 3rd one will later.

She remarked, "Can it really be this easy?" My response ... "the way you feel is the basis for your success. If you want to be successful you must feel successful. If you want to feel acquiring ideal prospects is effortless then you must feel that it is. When you commit to the feeling of already experiencing what you do want then you will magnetize that experience."

Here is another client story for you. This client had not yet charged a high-ticket price for his consulting services. He decided he would follow the game plan I laid out for him and was going to offer a program for $25,000.

I told him that if he was ready to do this he must feel like he already had clients at that price range. It was not enough to wish for these clients. He had to actually feel that he already had those clients. I encouraged him to continue thinking and feeling this way all the time. He began to do this consistently.

A few weeks later he had an inspired action which was to mention on Facebook that he was going to work with a private client for this amount. He received 4 direct messages on Facebook from people who were interested in working with him and 2 people hired him within 24 hours after posting this. Boom! $50,000 of new business by shifting his thoughts and feelings, following his own inner guidance system and taking action.

This is how manifesting and magnetizing works and it does work. You can direct your thoughts based on how they feel and little by little bring what you desire and deserve in your business and in your life and into your experience. I encourage you to begin to talk about what it is you want in your business and your life. Tell others and speak as if it has already happened.

Let me illustrate how this has made a real difference in my life. I started consulting, mentoring and coaching about 21 years ago. I have a friend who started within a week of me. When I only had one client in the very early days of my business, if you asked me how it was going I would say, "It is awesome. I am doing what I love and serving and helping and making a real difference".

I was, with one client. I believed I would be doing this with thousands and focused on that. 7 days after I started my business I had 15 clients and at the end of 30 days I had 30 clients, a huge corporate client, and a waiting list of clients... and I've never looked back.

If you asked my friend how she was doing when she also had 1 client she would have said, "It's really slow. I only have one client. It's going to be really hard to grow this business. I am struggling. No one knows what coaching is." Guess where her business is today? Sadly, she closed her doors after 14 months unable to get beyond 5 clients. She had the skills and the talent. She lacked the belief and right self-talk.

Whenever you speak the words, "I am" to the universe, think of them as if you have declared them to be true. I said, "I am doing what

I love..." and she said, "I am struggling". I know my clients are used to me correcting their language because it is so important to their success.

I want you to have what you want and you need to have someone help you with your mindset and your language. I believe we all need someone to regularly hear what we are saying to help us program more of the right self-talk until it becomes habit. In my experience, this isn't something one can do all by themselves.

Stand in your integrity and with your authenticity and truth. Do what you say you are going to do and be who you say you want to be. You are a powerful creator.

BECOME CONSCIOUS OF YOUR THOUGHTS

To make sure that your mind is really in a quiet place, notice your thoughts. Become aware of them, and learn to be able to decipher between the negative and the positive ones.

Don't try to push them away, because the more you try to push them away, the more they'll come. When your mind quiets, you can begin to attract the rest of the heart-based people who want to buy from you in an easy, effortless way.

If you are struggling with negative thoughts, ask yourself this question:

Is this true?

When I had left behind a very high-paying job as president of a national healthcare company, my thoughts went like this:

Wow, I quit this high-paying job and here I am starting a business with no income.

Well, if it doesn't work out, I can work at McDonald's and earn a living asking, "Do You want fries with that?"

Now, when I asked myself:

Is that true?

I realized it was ridiculous.

At the time, I had a Masters in Speech-Language Pathology, and I was in high demand.

They needed Speech-Language Pathologists and every day I got phone calls asking: "Could you work at this nursing home or hospital? Would you do healthcare for $60 an hour?"

So why would I be telling myself I'm doomed to "Do you want fries with that?"

I had to notice what my mind was saying, instead of pushing it away.

I had to notice it and ask myself:

Is this true?

Most of the time we find humor in it, and then we can say to our mind:

Shut up, mind! Shut up!

I don't want to listen to you.

You don't matter, and I'm going to go ahead and move forward without you.

Another great way to become conscious of your thoughts is to write them down. You can type them in a word document, or you can keep them in a journal. I recommend to clients that they hand-write in a journal, carry the journal around, and read those ideas every day. When you see them on the page, you can say:

Oh, here's that one.

Wow, that one's silly!

Get rid of it.

Oh, here's that one—that's a recurring theme.

That one comes up a lot.

Just notice them, recognize the patterns.

When you bring some consciousness and some awareness to your thoughts, then you can focus on them. You can fully focus on them with everything you've got. Really take a closer look at them and say:

Okay, I'm looking at you.

I'm looking at the thought that's coming up, that's creating some kind of resistance, some kind of doubt.

Instead of taking it as truth, say:

Interesting.

I'm aware of you.

There's something you want me to learn from this, and yet I know it's not true.

OK thought, I'm going to allow you to be in there.

And yet, I'm going to prove you wrong.

I'm going to go take an action or actions (physical actions, not just emotional) *to show you that you're not true.*

Void that negative thought right out of your mind.

TEST THAT YOUR INNER GAME IS WORKING

A few years ago, I had a client who told me he had mastered his inner game and I thought he hadn't. Instead of disagreeing with him I wanted him to prove to himself and to me that his inner game was on point. I told him a quick way to grow his business was to create a tribe of people who wanted to be connected to him because they felt drawn to him and that this happens when we oscillate the thoughts and beliefs of success he was claiming to have mastered.

I told him to go to where he believed his ideal qualified prospects would be hanging out. I wanted him to be with like-minded people who would believe in the success he was exuding and who held similar beliefs about their success. He joined a local group within about 10 days and told me the group was his exact target market and he was thrilled to be a part of the group.

After about a month he told me no one in the group was really connecting with him and he felt alone. I told him that was what I expected. He was shocked. I let him know I didn't think he mastered his self-talk. I believed he just kept trying to override it.

That means he still didn't believe in the success as if it was here and now. After a huge gulp, a big sigh came out. He said, "Got me, coach!". I was glad we agreed. We continued working on his self-talk and in a few more weeks he noticed the group was embracing him. No surprise there!

When you show up anywhere, if you are not believing in your own success people can see through you and they will tend to not want to do business with you. Imagine showing up at an in-person networking meeting, or virtual meeting or even on social media and not fully believing in your success.

As soon as people connect to that energy they will want to move in the other direction. Unless they, too, are unsuccessful and want to commiserate with you and that is the last type of person you want to form a relationship with.

People seek to be part of a tribe with other people they feel connected to.

If you want to have more clients then you will work on getting this inner game right before you run off to the land of outer actions. Otherwise, every connection you make with the wrong mind-set can actually repel prospects from you.

ALIGN YOURSELF WITH WHOM AND WHAT YOU WANT TO MAGNETIZE

I see another sad problem in marketing today that wastes a lot of time, energy, and money. It's that business owners don't truly know with whom they're supposed to be aligned.

Ask yourself: *What kind of person do I want to do business with?*

You don't want *everybody* to buy from you—if you do, you need to shift your thinking on that.

Acquiring customers will cost you a lot if you're trying to acquire everyone.

Ask yourself these questions:

- » What can I deliver in the marketplace?
- » Who would be interested in having what I deliver?
- » What kind of people would be interested?

If you're not aligned, you may be sending out a message that doesn't resonate at all.

Before working with me, one of my clients in the business of selling e-books and pamphlets was constantly sending out a message telling people that there were only a few particular titles available. After a while, people didn't believe that message. They came to know that the claim wasn't true.

My client was not attracting a lot of people, and the people he attracted weren't the most pleasant, easy, people to work with.

The client asked me: "Why is that?" "Why do I have difficult buyers?"

"Why do my buyers always want returns?"

It was very easy for me to see. My client wasn't aligned with their "who."

They needed to focus on:

- » Who do I want?
- » What do I stand for in the market?

They were attracting people who were giving the same kind of message as they were giving:

- » Here I am.

- » I'm not honest.
- » Come rip me off.

People would buy their e-books with a thirty-day guarantee. If they felt they didn't get their money's worth from their e-book, they could get their money back and, of course, keep the downloaded e-book. Most people I know who make that guarantee do not get a lot of people asking for returns. But this business owner had a *ton* of returns.

Why was this happening?

Because their offer wasn't in alignment. It was aligned with the people who were not ethical, who did not tell the truth. They would buy the e-book but then ask for a refund once they had the downloaded copy.

So, when you think about *exactly* who you want to market to, consider not only the demographic, but also the *psychographic*.

Notice and think about:

- » What your clients might eat
- » What they drink
- » Where they shop
- » What they like to smell
- » What they [prefer to] taste
- » How they live in society

Then strive to make sure you and your marketing messages are very aligned with them. Of course, your heart is going to reach them when you do this, because you're moving in a way that's heart to heart.

Then think about who they are:

- » See them
- » Feel them

» Notice them

Can you pick out your clients or customers if you walk into a room full of people?

I know, for example, that a majority of my clients like to eat Indian food. You might find that too detailed. But that's how well I know my marketplace.

I know that if the client comes to spend a day with me working on their business, that if at the end of the day, I invite them to an Indian restaurant, they're going to say yes and really appreciate the offer.

I know my clients that well.

Get aligned with your prospects and your clients on that level.

UNLEARN SELLING AND MARKETING

Traditional marketing and selling is dead.

People don't want to buy. They run away from buying in traditional, old sales-and-marketing approaches. They're tired of salespeople feeding them big hype, fancy stories, manipulating them, and overcoming objections. They also feel that if somebody—a company or individual—*needs* to market or sell a lot, that seller must not be very successful.

It's time for you to take a look at what you know about marketing: What do you believe about marketing?

What are the clichés? What are the patterns?

What is the thing that you think you must do in sales and marketing? Most likely, it's *not* what everybody else is doing.

Right now, in sales and marketing, a lot of business people try to attract sales by inflating their image.

"I'm great! I'm awesome! Come buy from my business! I'm not the only one who thinks I'm awesome, I have testimonials that say, 'Oh my gosh, I'm freakin' awesome!' Look! If you want to be awesome like me, if you want to have the figure or lifestyle I have, then you have to give me money. You have to buy my stuff."

Business people demand, "Give me money, be like me!" and use a ton of hype in their marketing. The good news is, the market itself is sick and tired of it. It hates hype—and so do I.

FOCUS ON THE CLIENT, NOT THE SELF

Hyping and inflating the self is the worst approach we've ever seen in sales history. Trying to sell to people by constantly talking at them and telling them how big our ego is does not work. I call it the guru-centric model - making ourselves significant.

When you make yourself, your business, your company, and your product as significant as calling yourself a guru, you actually turn people off. Instead of instilling confidence and making people exclaim "Wow!" they'll say "Ugh!"; it makes people want to run away. They won't have confidence in the business that is constantly yelling about how great it is.

The great news here is that once you unlearn all of these sales techniques—just dump them all out of your head—there's no pressure anymore. You don't have to do anything other than focus on how you are going to help people get whatever it is they want through your products or services.

People don't need to see anymore that you are awesome, that your product or service is cool or the best one out there. All you'll want to do now is show people who you are and let them have confidence in you.

Speak directly to your clients to tell them:
- » I've taken the time to study your industry.
- » I know where you're hurting.
- » You need help, and I know in what areas you need help.
- » I'm not going to agitate your problem. I'm going to do the opposite.

- » I'm here with my product or service to fix your problem.
- » Let me show you how I can help you.

Don't tell the clients that you're awesome and wonderful; tell them that you truly care about them and whatever it is that they want to receive by hiring you or buying from your company.

It's good news for you that so many other companies just don't get it. They're still selling and marketing, talking about their greatness, overcoming objections, and as a result, chasing people away.

Great—good for them! Let them do it that way, because they're sending the rest of the business right into your heart-based business.

In summary:

- » Focus on having a product or service that truly makes a difference in people's lives.
- » Decide to come from your heart.
- » Attract people with ease, instead of with selling.
- » Use the strategies I'm giving you in this chapter.

When you use these strategies, you become a magnet for your ideal customer. Clients will not only find you, they'll be really excited to do so. All the other businesses are doing something that turns them off. You'll be the person or business in greater demand. You'll be able to charge higher fees. Your competitors won't understand what hit them as you become the celebrity in your field.

Remember: in order to acquire more customers and create more revenue, you *have* to deliver. You must create that great experience for your clients, friends, and customers even before the sale ever happens.

Let go of all the things that you've learned about how to sell, and how to market, and embrace the knowledge that right now, you have the ability to benefit from everything your competitors are doing wrong.

- » Do everything right to show people that you really care about them.
- » Move yourself to celebrity status and watch as people line up to buy your products and services.
- » Remember to use reverse marketing.

Clients will be magnetically attracted through affinity marketing, and call out to you, "I want to use your products or services! Here I am."

SPEAKING TRUTH

In the first edition of *Turbocharge* I talked about not hyping, inflating and not pumping yourself up. Let me dive into this a bit more here.

I was speaking on stage for an event producer recently. I didn't know the producer very well, yet, I had heard from a friend who knew him, that he was struggling a bit financially and he was paying speakers their share of the products/services they sold at his events past the contracted payment date.

I stayed open, expected the best, was focused on finding only the positives about him, and delivering massive value to his audience. In the green room before I went on stage, he started tooting his own horn about his financial success, business success, and he even referred to himself as an "event genius".

Fast forward, I am on stage with less than 100 people in the audience and he had told me "all my events have at least 800 people in the room". After the event, he pays me over 14 days late, delaying the service I was providing to the 29 people who excitedly purchased and wanted to get going with me.

Event genius? I reached out to him and asked to have a 10-minute de-brief call. Me, being me and coming from love, truth, transparency, authenticity and genuinely wanting to help him I said, "It seems to me

CHAPTER ONE - THE EXPANDED HEART-REPRENEUR® PHILOSOPHY

like you might need some help filling seats and creating more financial success with your event model. Is this accurate?".

He then confided the truth to me. If he had asked me to speak and told me his situation I would still have spoken for him and would have a lot more respect for how he did business. Heart-repreneurs do business from a place of truth.

My point? Act as if you have what you do want and don't exaggerate or tell false tales. I made a big mistake in my business doing this and will pull back the curtain and share very transparently with you. Back over a decade a TV host called me "The Guru of Coaching". I thought that sounded pretty cool. I trademarked the term and began using it and having people refer to me that way.

One day I had an epiphany and decided I didn't resonate with that term. Was I really a guru? Was I the only coach on the planet? It was a bunch of hype and not in alignment with how I wanted people to experience me. I let it go and asked people to no longer call me a guru.

Speak truth. Be humble. Don't over-promise - in fact make no promises and just deliver for the sake of delivering. This is how Heart-repreneurs roll.

Are you starting to see yourself Turbocharging your business the Heart-repreneur® way?

I'm glad to have this opportunity to expand what was in the first edition. Wait till you see what is coming! Here we go!

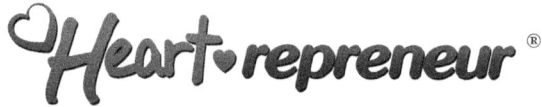

DID YOU KNOW THE HEART-REPRENEUR® TEAM WILL GIVE YOU PERSONAL ADVICE?

As a reader and fellow Heart-repreneur® you can schedule a phone consult with our team. This session is your Turbocharge business game plan. We will go very deep into your business and sort out and solve your business problems. We will expose any overlooked problems and use Terri›s decades of experience to share tools, tips and strategies with you.

Your session will deep dive anything and everything related to your business and can include: lead generation, your online and offline sales process, increasing conversions without selling, your business model, marketing tactics, business operations and anything else business related you choose.

This is a very focused session customized and designed so you walk away with a game plan to fix what isn't quite yet right in your business and will set you up for a great future from a highly regarded business growth strategist who does business as a Heart-repreneur®.

Because you are a reader of this book you can schedule your session now.

If you are serious about turbocharging your business and want Terri's help as someone who has guided the success of over 5,000 other business owners, entrepreneurs and marketers for many decades and believe her real-world experience and Heart-repreneur® style can help you grow your business then grab this opportunity to get a personal consult. This session is yours to ask specific questions, to pick our brains and get advice, information, and knowledge to help you grow your business.

https://www.heart-repreneur.com/new-strategy-session-page

CHAPTER TWO

• • • • • • • • • • •

LEAVE THE PAST IN THE PAST

FORGET EVERYTHING YOU KNOW ABOUT SALES AND MARKETING RIGHT NOW!

STOP MARKETING AND SELLING AT PEOPLE

Most businesses tend to market by telling people how great they are, talking about what gurus they are, and sharing why they are the best company regardless of the product or service. Their marketing style is chasing and telling people.

When people are being chased and spoken at by businesses, potential customers will face the other direction. At this time, people really don't want to be marketed *to* or marketed *at*, so the shift is now about finding a way to attract and magnetize people who will find you and simply ask what you're selling.

GIVE THEM A TASTE SO THEY'LL FALL IN LOVE WITH YOU

Some businesses use high-pressure tactics, try to overcome objections, or resort to manipulation, but these are undesirable ways to attract business. These tactics make it more difficult to sell. What's easier and works really well is when you give people a taste of what they're getting. Give them a bit of a show that encourages them—if they're the right people—to have a greater desire to buy your product or service.

After they've tasted it, they come in and buy because they don't feel a risk. Giving them a taste takes away their fear of being sold to and manipulated.

One of the best working examples of giving people a taste is the ice cream store Baskin-Robbins. You can go in and try a sample. They report that 100 percent of the people who do a taste test go ahead and buy ice cream. It would just make sense; no matter what business you offer, let people try it. Let them decide if they like it, and if they want to buy.

When you stop marketing *at* people, you will become more magnetic. Your ideal prospects and your ideal customers are tired of hype and overblown claims and promises. They're running away from sales pressure. The best way to turn people into customers is not use hype or send cookie-cutter emails, phone calls or letters. Just allow people to get a feel for who you are, what you do, and in a non-threatening sales manner, allow them to gravitate towards you.

PINK SPOONS OPEN HEARTS MAKE IT EASY TO TRY YOU ON

Many years ago, I worked scooping ice cream for Baskin-Robbins. I was fascinated with the little pink spoons of samples we gave out. People came in, tasted a few flavors and always decided to buy ice cream.

I teach all business owners to use this pink spoon approach to marketing. Start people off with the free taste. In my case a valuable educational webinar (https://www.heart-repreneur.com/master-class). After that, we give them a 10-minute free consult that is all value and zero selling.

If you want to get even more value and to get a lot of tools, tips, strategies, and techniques, you can then set up a full 90-minute customized game plan session with me for a very low fee which can be used toward any of my programs.

From there they can enter my 6-week, *Ultimate System to Attract High Ticket Clients Who Love You* course, and if it's a fit, they can then join my one year mentoring program. Beyond that, they can ask to work with me for private consultations.

By having various levels, people can do a taste test and move up through the levels as it makes sense. I don't try to sell them the full ice cream sundae. Never. I have them try a sample and then have a bigger taste and then more deliciousness, if they desire.

I don't give away my 90-minute game plan as a taste test, just like the ice cream store didn't give away a scoop or a cone. I move people slowly through this, helping them with what they want and need, and letting them know what isn't a fit for them as well.

I recommend your pink spoon be automated and be a webinar, because my clients and I are knocking it out of the park with this. People are tired of audios, ebooks and reports. Webinars are hot. Keep it valuable. Make it educational, fun and interesting. Let the webinar work for you 24 hours a day, 7 days a week. Then sit back with pink spoons of taste tests going out and ideal clients rolling in.

I have used videos, audios, quizzes, assessments, emails, books, special reports and tickets to events and can tell you that in every case my automated webinar wins. It brings me the most qualified leads every single day.

When you offer something after the pink spoon that you are going to enroll people in, such as my: *Ultimate System to Attract High Paying Clients Who Love You Program,* I want you to offer them a package that allows you to automate a lot of what you say or do every day over and over again with clients.

We give away a course valued at $5,000 for free as our pink spoon. Enroll at https://gethotpayingclients.com/.

Here is how I shifted a client to do exactly this.

My client is a weight loss consultant. She was telling people to eat the same things over and over again every single day and charging for individual sessions. She was earning under $60,000 a year and spending hours and hours speaking to clients and constantly creating content. She was blogging, podcasting, posting on social media, appearing as a guest on tele-summits, holding live events, networking, and more. She was tired and her business had not grown in the 5 years she had been at it.

I helped her set up her automated educational webinar and put an end to all other content creation so leads could flow in. I had her create a high-ticket group coaching program to get her clients the result of shedding 10 pounds or more by following a fun, easy and simple weight loss program where they would never feel deprived. The value of people losing this weight was easily worth thousands of dollars to them.

She decided to charge $2,700 per person and she guaranteed if they followed her program they would lose weight. Every week they got a customized eating plan sent to them automatically, a customized work out automatically sent to them and they got a 45-minute group coaching call to help them achieve their goals. They also were part of a Facebook forum to watch additional pre-recorded videos and to gain access to community support.

It would take her about 2 hours a week to deliver this program. Not 40 or more hours a week. The first time she offered the program she only got 4 people registered. I pointed out that 4 people at $2,700 each meant she spent 12 hours and earned $900 per hour and she earned $10,800 in 6 short weeks. She celebrated those numbers.

The second time she offered the program she had case studies from the first group and it was easy to get ideal prospects interested. She had 9 people in the second group. That was $24,300 in income and now she was earning $2,025 per hour! Can you see how her income increased while she created huge value for clients and how she was leveraging her time?

Every client she enrolled was accepted into the program because she knew she could deliver the result they needed. She wasn't trying to sell them anything. She wanted to deliver the results to them. She put them in this program versus doing hourly consulting rates and they stayed and got results.

In the past, people would start with her consulting and often drop out. There was no package. There was no commitment. They didn't pay enough to have a commitment to losing the weight. They weren't serious. They weren't ideal clients.

This became what she offered people. A package they could commit to and get great results from. After this package if they wanted more she could talk to them about the next level. She wasn't trying to move them up. She wanted to keep them as her family members and give them whatever results they were seeking.

DO A GOOD JOB OF EDUCATING BUYERS

Instead of talking at people and throwing products and services in your prospect's face, it's much better to have a taste test. That way, they get to educate themselves.

They get to decide: *I want to try that pink spoon of mint chocolate chip ice cream. I want to see if it's good enough that I want to enjoy the whole thing.*

You're not coming at potential customers; you're attracting them. You're allowing them to have a taste test without giving them any pressure or any reason not to go any further with you. You're not even going to tell them how great you are, how wonderful your product is, or brag about your features and benefits. This is contrary to everything you've learned about selling.

Instead, you're going to let them create their own sales process by arriving at their own idea that they want what you have.

I love to use Apple as an example. Apple doesn't have to try to sell you the new iPhone. They don't have to announce that it's better than the last one because people just line up the day it comes out.

That's what we are trying to create: people coming to you.

It would be wonderful for people to line up saying, "I know I want it. Tell me how I can get it.

Here's my money."

That's what you're going for, for your customers to want to come to you.

ALLOW PEOPLE TO GET A SENSE OF YOU

Instead of trying to sell people, allow them to convert themselves into buying and ask to buy from you. Once people see, and hear you they can get a sense of you and begin to see if they oscillate with you. If you aren't allowing them to try you on and to get to know you then they will not be ready to ask to buy your products or services.

One way you can do this is with the homepage of your website where the about me page truly gives them a deep look at who you are and what you stand for. Then offer them from your website a way to sign up for a workshop, automated webinar, free class, gift, e-book, audio or video, where they can begin to get a good idea of who you are, what your gifts and results are, and what it is like to experience you.

Everything you do online and offline needs to have your clear Core Unique Positioning Statement as part of it. You may offer people different ways to get results with you, such as: an online class, a live event, a webinar, a coaching program, a membership site, etc.

It is important that you develop systems that make it safe for people to check you out from a safe distance. This allows them to slowly get closer to you and opt-in to be in touch with you. I think of people as hiding below an iceberg and not wanting to be seen. You want them to begin to raise their hand a little above the iceberg until they are ready to stand up and allow you to embrace them.

CHAPTER TWO - LEAVE THE PAST IN THE PAST

Be certain that you have a great Core Unique Positioning Statement so people can be attracted to you. This is how you sort and sift the right people who may have some interest in you and the outcomes you deliver. As you continue building a relationship by giving those who follow you online and offline valuable educational content and build a relationship with those prospects, some of them will sift themselves into wanting more of you and your services.

Some will sift themselves away from you as they are not qualified prospects. What's left? The ones who know they want to have your services or products. They will separate themselves and ask to buy from you.

Most entrepreneurs are focused only on getting new clients. That's a mistake. It's harder to have a new prospect quickly say yes than it is for an existing client to come back for another one of your services or products. Let me share a client story with you so you can really grasp the importance of this idea.

My client is a hair salon owner who charges about $100 for a new style. She was doing Groupon's and coupons and spending a lot of money on ads and direct mail. I had her stop all of that and instead focus on bringing her clients in more frequently, and going to past clients and reactivating them. Instead of clients coming 4 times a year for three years, $1,200 (her average), we focused on having them come more frequently.

She changed her average for those clients to 6 times a year (predicting a 3-year average) so she now was making $1,800 per client which is $600 more for every current client. Then we recalled past clients and gave them a special enticement to return and she added 11 former clients back to her salon. If they average the same as her current clients (which is our expectation), then she will bring in $19,800 just in recalled clients.

This is a much better and faster way to generate revenue than hunting for new clients. On top of that we have added additional services so she will soon be averaging $125 per client and we added a referral reward program. So far, she has 9 new clients as a result of that - valued at $16,200!

Her current clients feel she is very attentive because her salon isn't doing a lot of marketing for new people, she is just focusing on making them look and feel their best!

THE CONFUSED MIND SAYS NO

When a prospect is checking out your services and products you must remember that the confused mind says no. If they aren't sure what you are offering or what the experience will be like or what the end result will be, they just say no and move on.

One of my clients had a confusing website, confusing social media messages and lacked a Core Unique Positioning Statement. He is a family therapist specializing in children with anxiety disorders. I changed all his social media with his Core Unique Positioning Statement and created a website that was simple.

The site told what he was about and then offered them an opt-in to watch the 45-minute webinar I helped him create which showed parents 5 things they could do quickly to decrease the anxiety their children were experiencing.

That webinar plays 24-7 and his current patients share the webinar with others. At the close of the webinar he offers a 10-minute Zoom meeting with the parents to discuss their individual questions. Leads come in every day because his message is clear and his audience understands what actions to take.

Once they watch the webinar they experience him and began a relationship with my client and then those who reach out are able to have a deeper experience of him. It's easy for them to convert themselves into clients. His social media, emails, business card and flyers, drive everyone to one action - go to my website and watch this educational webinar that will help you help your child.

The webinar gives them help and the answers they seek. It is a gift that he invites people to watch that attracts high quality prospects to him every day. This entire process helps prospects have clarity and draws in people who resonate with his message.

If people come to your social media pages, your website, pick up your flyer or business card and there are many things to select from, they will move along to someone else. They won't develop a relationship with you. This is why you must have a website and a webinar that speaks to your target audience, pulls them in, gives them clarity about who you are, what you do, and what they can expect from you.

If you are doing the work you love and not getting the prospects you desire, then you need to look at your Core Unique Positioning Statement, your online messages including website and social media, email and your offline messages including what you say at networking meetings, all printed materials and all other forms of communication.

Your message must be attractive to your ideal prospects, you must be excited about your website and your webinar. Be proud that it is high value and helps your ideal prospects. Your website and your webinar are your two core marketing pieces. You don't need a beautiful website. You need one that resonates with words, images and videos with your audience so that once they see the homepage they decide to opt-in to your webinar. That's it.

All I care about when I do website reviews for my clients is that the home page is solid, not confusing and drives ideal prospects to opt-in for your webinar. The home page is about the prospect and helps them to get a result and an experience. Don't make the home page about you. People should feel at home when they are on your home page.

If they want to know about you, they can go to your about page that has your bio next. Keep in mind people do business with someone they know, like and trust.

You only have three seconds to grab the attention of people when they come to your website. Your home page must be about them and their experience. Show them you understand their pain and have an educational webinar that can bring them a result, that will help them to achieve their goal and/or overcome their pain.

Be sure to use a friendly photo of you on the home page and a video so they can experience you. Look at my home page at https://heartrepreneur.com/ as an example. Remember, confused people say no. Compel them so they can feel your passion and enthusiasm and get a sense of who you are.

Have your Core Unique Positioning Statement on the home page so they get a sense of who you are, what you are about, and how you are different. No jargon at all on the page. Nothing that can even slightly confuse them.

I saw a site the other day for a financial coach and the home page had terms like "fiscal" "economic security" "transformation" "manage expectations" "risk aversion" "asset allocation"... not clear at all and very abstract.

This will confuse prospects and certainly not command their attention nor convert them to want to know more.

HOME PAGE SIMPLIFIED

On your home page, in writing and by short video, communicate what results you get for which types of people who have what kinds of problems. Then share a case study of a typical client or have a client share their own success. This is how you command attention and compel people to opt-in to watch your webinar or whatever lead magnet you decide on.

Your case study should show how you helped your client solve their problem. This should be the exact type of client you want to attract with the same or similar type of problem. People will live vicariously through your case study and relate to that person's story.

Remember, all we are trying to do is to get people to raise their hands and begin to magnetize towards you. Nothing more.

SHARE YOUR GIFTS INSTEAD OF FLASHING CREDENTIALS

Many people mistakenly think talking about their credentials and trying to make themselves sound wonderful is the way to go. I think that is the number one mistake that people are making.

Almost nobody buys because of your credentials.

There are plenty of successful people who lack credentials. Bill Gates didn't have any credentials. He dropped out of college, and he founded Microsoft. We could have just said that Bill Gates is the guy who founded Microsoft and he's a nobody, but he's a somebody.

Look at Mark Zuckerberg; he co-founded Facebook. We don't care what his credentials are. He doesn't need credentials.

And of course, Steve Jobs didn't have credentials; he also was a college dropout.

You can make people very interested in your products and services without having to have credentials or turning yourself into some kind of a guru.

All you need to do is:

» Offer what people want.
» Provide a way for them to taste it.
» Leave time and space for them to come to their own decision: I like it.
» Make it easy and effortless for them to purchase your product or service.

Forget turning yourself or your company into a guru, and forget even listing your credentials. Potential customers do not pay attention to credentials.

Stop marketing and selling at people; you really want to become a partner, a co-creator, in the sales process. You're not directing the process—you're not even coaching it. You're sitting with your client the way an instructor does in a driver's education car, not even as driver and passenger. You're *both* sitting in the driver's seat. If your client wants to step on the gas pedal, you're there. The car doesn't crash, just like in driver's ed. You can help them.

That's your *only purpose*. When you stop trying to come *at* people and partner *with* people, you'll create more sales.

DO SOMETHING THAT LETS PEOPLE FIND YOU

If you want people to be able to try you on then you must be doing some marketing. A friend of mine messaged me the other day and told me she decided she didn't want to market her business. She just wanted to do the healing and use her gift to heal people. I told her she had three choices that I could see.

One, she could get a business partner who would do the marketing; two she could close her doors and get a job, or three she could stop resisting marketing and embrace allowing people to find her and her gifts and get the help they were seeking.

This holds for you, as well. Your responsibility, in my view, is to make sure people can discover what you offer so they can engage you for the results they are craving. It's selfish of you not to market what can help others. I am suggesting a marketing path that is easy, effortless, automated, non-sales-like, and that is proven to work.

If you learn this information and do nothing with it, then you will have decided this book is a shelf-help book to sit on your shelf and collect dust. I hope you are going to make a transformation with this material and not just digest my information. I want this book to be a self-help book that you actually get results with.

As long as you are marketing from an authentic place and can deliver the outcomes you say you can bring, all is well. Pick marketing actions that resonate with you and then go do them.

One of my clients decided he really liked to do events. He decided to host an event teaching people how to get their first 5 clients online. He joined a hub and gave out master passes to attend the event for free.

He also sent out an email to his list and shared on social media. He did a few Facebook Lives to provide content and generate interest, too. He was making it easy for his ideal qualified prospects to find him.

You can do any marketing activity that resonates with you. Some examples are:

- Write articles
- Blog
- Social media
- Host a tele-summit
- Google or Facebook ads
- Write press releases
- Give interviews
- Host a podcast
- Go to local community meetings and events
- Host an event
- Sponsor an event
- Free automated webinar
- Joint venture marketing
- Email marketing
- Direct mail
- Newsletter
- Post flyers
- Run a contest
- Give away coupons
- Give referral rewards

And on and on and on! I don't want you to use all of these things. I want you to pick 3-5 that resonate with you as being fun and authentic. Just do some things. You cannot rely on word of mouth hoping people will hear about you.

BUILDING YOUR TRIBE

What I am about to reveal can easily double the number of clients you now have and is some of the most powerful information that will truly turbocharge your business success. Best of all, it is built on nothing more than connecting with people heart to heart.

Imagine spending less time, energy, and money marketing, and finally having a business built on money rolling in and freedom rolling out. See yourself enjoying your free time, your family, your vacations and working a lot less hours while making a lot more money.

Remember I told you to forget what you believe or think you know about sales and marketing, right? I mean it. I don't want you to buy into the hype that you can sit at home in your underwear and use the Internet only to build your business. That isn't very connected.

In fact, while people can do business by clicking all over the place, Heart-repreneurs set themselves apart by doing business face to face. People want to be with people. That is fact. Human beings crave real relationships. They want contact and connection and to see each other eye to eye and to feel each other heart to heart.

While I work with clients all over the world and meet a large number of prospects on the Internet, I spend the bulk of my time connecting with people face to face. Why? Almost all successful business owners first get known in their own communities and then expand outwards. I appreciate my community for getting me known in the Philadelphia area for my business strategies and I will always give back to my local community.

You must include local marketing in your activities because that is where and how you truly make connections. You know that people do

CHAPTER TWO - LEAVE THE PAST IN THE PAST

business with people they know, they like and they trust, right? Well, this happens a heck of a lot faster when people experience you in person versus online.

Here is an actual scenario from my business. I recently conducted a one day Coaching Intensive (https://www.heartrepreneuracademy.com/event-main/) sharing marketing secrets and helping the audience customize and implement them in their business. There were about 40 people in attendance. After those people got to experience me and we connected in person, 12 of them hired me in some capacity.

Why? I gave them a taste of the kinds of skills I had and they viewed me as someone who could help them. They decided on their own that they wanted more of what I offer. It is so much easier to gain clients and to retain them long-term when you have a real in-person connection.

This is exactly how I established my consulting and mentoring business a few decades ago. I helped a lot of people in my local community face to face and they hired me. The other benefit of doing business this way is that you become seen as an expert while you are creating a community in your backyard.

People began to talk about me. A buzz got generated. Soon, I was being requested to speak at local events, and getting hired by local organizations and by local business owners.

I still do live events to this day. Why? I enjoy connecting with people, being a part of my local community, and I make a great income while having a ton of fun.

Too many mentors, consultants and coaches aren't giving this type of marketing guidance and many of them are fake experts who don't have the results they want either.

Let me draw out a big distinction before we go deeper. I am not talking about networking. The word itself sounds like "hard work" to me and sounds very outcome driven. I am talking about truly creating a tribe through connection based marketing.

Think about any networking event you have recently been to. You go hoping to find someone to do business with, right? You receive and hand out a bunch of cards or force yourself to give a referral at a leads group and get a crummy lead or two a month from the group, yet, you keep going back to the meetings. If those resonate with you then go.

I only go where I can serve qualified prospects and marketing partners. I spend my time with people who are very likely to buy my services and products and to also refer me to others who would be interested in the benefits I provide.

How do I achieve all of this? Better yet, how can YOU achieve all of this?

Easy! Pick a local group you resonate with so that you can connect at least once a month and generate revenue and serve people long-term.

Before we get into a specific action plan keep a few things in mind.

Most people do marketing all wrong. They spend a lot of time, energy, and money creating logos, business cards, and flyers. Posting on social media, and hiding behind their desktops. They really aren't marketing, they don't like the idea of marketing, and don't feel it fits their personality. Some people don't want to do marketing because it feels gross to them and others think that as a transformed and conscious human being marketing doesn't fit for them.

Heart-repreneurs market correctly. We market because we strongly believe in the service we provide. We know we make a big difference in the lives and businesses of those we are called to serve. We realize, if we didn't get out and share what we do, we would have no clients to impact, and therefore would be out of business serving no one.

Keep this in mind. People have problems and need solutions. If you have a solution for them it is your responsibility to make sure people know about it and that is done through marketing. The reason you market is to help people find their solutions.

I am talking about marketing with truth and integrity. Can I help this person? If I can, let me share what I have for them. If I can't, let me see

CHAPTER TWO - LEAVE THE PAST IN THE PAST

if I can refer them elsewhere or let them know I am not the person to help them.

When you get active in your local community and you select the organization or group you want to network with do it from a place of love and contribution. Just know that local marketing works and is very powerful. When people get to experience you and what you do, they can begin to decide if what you offer is a match for them or not. Remember, you want to be known for one result you create for the clients you work with.

In your community, you can host an event (even if you aren't a speaker I can show you how to do this with ease), invite your new network to attend and get a lot of clients from this.

I have a very introverted client who started following this process about 6 months ago and at her last 2-hour event where she had 22 people she sold $42,000!

Just start hanging out with your tribe, going to their events, and then invite them to something that will give them a result they need, that you can deliver. Create massive value for them. Invite them to work with you further. Offer a program, service or product. Watch them happily engage and invest because they see you have the solution they need.

Let me share another idea that is fun and propelled my business in the early days. I invited prospects to my home for a party. It had a murder mystery theme to make it really fun. We connected and had a ton of fun at my home playing this murder mystery game. It was zero pressure. Prospects began to ask me questions about my business and I answered them with no hype. Within 26 days of the party I had picked up about $5,000 in revenue.

One of my clients took this idea and hosted a party with a different theme for people from her networking group. She did over $11,000 of business with those people, only 6 days after the event! Neither of us sold or hosted these parties with any attachment to an outcome other than connecting with people and having fun.

Meetups are an inexpensive, easy and effortless way to find clients and to bring local prospects together. Just go over to www.meetup.com, create a group that targets the outcome you deliver for ideal prospects, and then hold a local event for people who want that outcome.

One of my clients hosts a Meetup every single month for entrepreneurs who provide services to homeowners. She attracts members who have that interest and has gotten a steady stream of clients just by hosting the meetings each month.

Being at the hub of a networking meeting like I am or like my client is, is a great marketing strategy. We get to spend time with people we really like and want to connect with. We have a lot of fun and provide value and magic happens.

This local marketing model is simple, easy and works because you go to meetings, or host your own, show up being genuine and enthusiastic, and simply connect with people. No agenda. No sales and marketing training or thoughts in mind. Connection for the sake of connecting and nothing more.

Connecting is a natural people skill. I don't need to show you how to do this. Just be fully present in the moment. Come from a place of caring and love, to help and to add value. Nothing more is necessary. Your entire focus with marketing and selling is to forget everything anyone ever taught you, told you or that you read about. Just dump all of this out of your head and focus on serving the other person.

What has happened for my clients who have followed this advice is that they have become known as the go-to expert in their local area. They have a steady stream of qualified leads and new clients every month. They have established a community of raving fans. They love marketing now because it feels good, is aligned with who they are and how they like to do business.

They are simply spending time with people they enjoy. They are actually supporting their local community, making a difference by doing great work, and providing value and outcomes. They have generated a lot of buzz around their businesses. This allows them to fill their events, sell their programs, services, and products with ease.

They have greatly increased their income by attending one meeting or hosting one meeting per month, and have cut down marketing time and marketing expense by using these local marketing methods that are proven to work.

Picture yourself being seen as the local go-to expert while positively impacting your local community. I urge you to connect with your local community right away. They need what you have and what you can bring to them. Bring your expertise to them and serve them.

PLEASE YOUR TRIBE

To command, connect and convert you must lead people and share your message with those who need and want to hear your message. It is not to change people who don't resonate with your message to decide that they will shift and follow you and your message. That is selling and not the way a Heart-repreneur® does business. Your job is easy. You offer people what it is they want to buy and be certain you are visible so they can find you.

People join your tribe or community if they are oscillating at a similar frequency. Today people have so many choices. You don't need to convince them, sell them or manipulate them to join you. You connect with the right people and soon you are creating a movement with them.

This has happened with my own Heart-repreneur® movement where like-minded people connected with me and now are creating value for others in the tribe.

Whatever you care the most about and have the most passion for is what your tribal movement is based on. How can you get your tribe built and people connected with your mission?

Here are some of the things my clients have done with my help:

- » Created a support group
- » Formed a study club
- » Created a networking group
- » Started programs, workshops and hosted events
- » Sent out newsletters
- » Hosted teleseminars and webinars
- » Created a Facebook group
- » Had a social event

Doing what is fun for you, how can you get the like-minded people together either virtually or in person?

This client story might inspire you to come up with some ideas.

My client is a realtor who strongly believes in creating green communities. She decided to host a small event for local homeowners to teach how to have a greener environment at work and at home. She hosted this event at the local library. People met and networked for a bit and then she shared her top 12 green living tips.

She gave away the list laminated on hard card stock to all attendees. After the short event, people continued to mingle. As the leader of this event with people who were already like-minded, some of them were interested in buying homes, some in selling, and many knew other people who might be. She created value and began this community group.

She held the meeting again 6 weeks later and encouraged all members to invite other people. The group grew from 8 to 15 the next time. She also started a Facebook group for the same audience and topic, and has begun a green movement in her local community. People from this community are coming to her for her business services as a realtor as a side benefit.

Yes, this is how it works!

WORD OF MOUTH SPREADS YOUR MOVEMENT

Word of mouth marketing happens when your community or tribe start talking about what you do and who you are. A buzz gets created that others are carrying on for you.

What creates word of mouth marketing? First, a message that people connect to that is simple for them to share with others.

One of my clients offers people a free sample of her homemade chocolates and says, "Tell any of your friends that if they want the best homemade chocolate all they have to do is ask me." She has a great product. People have shared her product very quickly, and she has a community getting her movement out that is based on people getting the best chocolate on the planet, without having to pay a lot to enjoy it.

I must say that anyone who has tried her chocolate can't stop raving about it. Wouldn't it be awesome if your clients were all sharing you with their friends and your business was growing from word of mouth marketing?

Take some time to think about how people experience you and your business. What can excite them to talk to people about their experience? What feels like it would be fun for you to create as an experience people would be excited to share with others? You want to create contagious energy about you and your service or product. If it is fun and exciting you want to repeat that experience for people over and over again.

I had this experience with a local restaurant. The first time I went, the manager came over and chatted with me. We got into a conversation about social media. A few minutes later he sent a complimentary appetizer to our table.

I returned a few weeks later, the manager walked over to my table and told me how happy he was to see me again. He chatted with all my guests. He sent over samples of the drink of the day. Because he was making the experience fun and I was digging it, I soon found myself telling others to go to this restaurant and so did those who I brought with me.

I didn't have to know his Core Unique Positioning Statement to share positive word of mouth. I was happy to tell people, "Do you know the restaurant called Smokey Bones? You just have to go. You won't believe what the manager there will do for you when you go! He is filled with free surprises every time."

People remember this, they go and then they tell their friends to go also. Pretty soon Smokey Bones was growing from our viral word of mouth.

Just remember to create an experience people will talk about, enjoy, and that is fun for you. Do something you will truly love doing. Let people talk about that because it leaves a memorable impression on them. Do the unexpected. Create experiences where you and your business are being talked about and shared by others in a positive way.

CREATE FUN AND SPREAD HAPPINESS

I believe owning your own business is fun, brings pleasure and enjoyment, and that you will want to be a Heart-repreneur® business if serving clients is something you do that makes you happy. To me, that is the only purpose of being in business, the only way to be in business, and only reason to be in business.

When I am connected to my purpose, delighted to be doing what I love and helping clients, then money is rolling in and freedom is rolling out with no effort.

I helped one of my clients make this shift. She came to me after spending 2 years struggling to make enough money and attract enough clients to her Law of Attraction coaching program. I simply had her start focusing on doing the activities she loved with the people she loved, finding ways to share her value and spread her joy.

After 4 months of being happy and spending time with the people who were her tribe, she had a full client schedule, had appeared on 2 radio shows, 1 tele-summit and was going to be speaking at a local event.

Her clients were raving about their experiences with her because they could feel her heart, her love, and her joy in working with them and helping them. She is a perfect example of what it means to be a Heart-preneur®.

NO MORE BUSINESS AS USUAL

People are tired of being manipulated, lied to and mistreated. They want to do business with people and companies that are kind, in integrity, authentic, transparent and that don't use slick marketing techniques.

People want to have real heart-based relationships, not based on profits; out of honesty, integrity and transparency, not lies, hype and/or manipulation. They want win-win exchanges and not win-lose exploitation; and they want to do business with people who have a love of life, not a love of money.

STOP USING TRADITIONAL MARKETING MEDIA

Traditional marketing media does not work; it's expensive. There's very little direct mail that's even looked at. It's reaching people who don't necessarily have a desire and haven't raised their hand, so it's a waste of your money.

Traditional marketing media, like advertising, does not work. They have been *shown* not to work.

People see so many messages a day that they don't pay attention to advertising messages, particularly in print.

The traditional ways of advertising that shove promotions *at* people are absolutely a waste of your time, money, energy, and creativity. Skip the print ads, telephone calls (which people just don't answer anymore and certainly don't like), and shoving things *at* people.

You won't need to ask whether they're your target audience. You won't need to ask if they want your product. They'll tell you.

ADVERTISING DOESN'T WORK

We are being constantly bombarded by advertisements these days. Advertising does not work through:

- » Email
- » Ads in e-zines
- » Direct mail of postcards or flyers
- » Any form of traditional visual advertising

These methods totally fail, and here's why: people are getting tired of email. Email doesn't necessarily reach the people it's supposed to reach, and often, people don't open their emails. So, you might be sending out a lot of email but it will get you no response.

We have the same problem with direct mail. A lot of people do not look at direct mail if it seems like advertising. As an example, right here today on my desk, I have three items that came in the mail. I've not opened any of them; they all look like ads. They'll be in the circular file, wasting the advertiser's money.

If we look at advertising in newspapers, or radio, or television, or in any form of print, it's usually saying how great the advertiser is.

"I'm great! I'm advertising! I'm wonderful!"

People don't tend to buy because of that. They only buy when they hear about real results, not about how great you are. So, none of these forms of advertising will work, and they will cost a lot of money and energy.

The number of ads that people are faced with every day is overwhelming:

- » You drive down the road and there are billboards.
- » There are trucks with ads.
- » There are ads in your home.

- » There are newspapers, magazines, television, and Pandora.
- » Then on top of that, you go to the internet, and your Facebook is filled with ads.
- » Your Gmail is full of ads.

Ads are everywhere. We tend to stop looking at ads.

So now you must train your brain to think differently in order to reach your target audience.

JOINT VENTURE AND AFFILIATE MARKETING: NOT VERY EFFECTIVE

Over the last fifteen years, affiliate marketing and joint venture marketing became very popular. Business people were excited; they thought that they could begin to use other companies' lists, or other people's buyers, and get their product or service in front of those buyers.

Joint ventures and affiliates are very similar. It's a collaboration in which, for example, the massage therapy place and the hair salon down the street have a reciprocal deal. When someone comes in for a massage, they get a coupon for a haircut down the street, say, five dollars off. When they get the haircut, they get a coupon for five dollars off a massage.

It sounds wonderful. But what we're finding is that customers typically won't use those coupons; they won't even pick them up. They'd rather not be tied between businesses giving back and forth to each other in a financial way, or even if it's not financial. It's perception.

Frankly, consumers have gotten wise. Customers see that something's being promoted to them, and that the vendor is telling them it's wonderful and a great deal. We as customers get suspicious. They suspect there's got to be some reason the seller is trying so hard to pitch the product or service.

Consumers began to guess that there must be a financial payoff.

When you open your audience to another business, you should have a reason to do so and your audience needs to know what that reason is.

They have every right to ask why you are opening them to this other product or service. That's something for which your clients need more justification, rather than you telling them it's good, no matter how much they like, know, and trust you. They need that pink-spoon experience of getting a taste.

EMAIL AND DIRECT MAIL: ALSO INEFFECTIVE

People are inundated with email. It's a huge complaint in our society today. There's too much of it. You may be sending out wonderful emails. They could be very valuable. But if the emails ever make it through the many filters, they sit in the inbox. People usually don't look at them. We've gone into companies where people have five, ten—and for one lady just last week—twelve thousand emails in her inbox. Twelve *thousand*!

So, your email isn't necessarily going to get a response. It certainly is not going to create a purchase. I would highly recommend re-thinking using email, although it's free and seems like a good way to advertise. Instead, text people or pick up the phone. People respond to other people, not clicking from place to place or email to email.

The alternative idea that many people have is that using direct mail may work better, because there isn't much of it anymore. You may think that other than people getting their bills and their flyers for shopping, there's not a lot of direct mail, so you'll stand out.

Well, that doesn't work anymore either. People know that direct mail is filled with reviews about yourself, and they don't trust what you're saying. You're not a credible expert; you're just showing up in their home or their office, and they didn't invite you in. That's what direct mail looks and sounds like.

Direct mail can be expensive; it used to have a return on investment of about one percent. Nowadays it's about 0.1 percent. I would recommend, again, that you stop using these traditional methods. Text people and call them. Those are the two better choices and of those, the phone is number one.

PRINT MARKETING: A WASTE OF MONEY

People have spent a lot of money doing print marketing using:

» Business cards
» Flyers
» Letterheads
» Brochures
» Postcards

I've seen so many people print ads and flyers and just hand them out. I'm going to tell you that it's very expensive to do print marketing so it looks nice and it represents your brand.

People don't trust promotional material that's printed.

When you print something, it's another form of self-advertisement, saying: "I'm great! I'm wonderful! My company is amazing! Come here!"

People don't trust when you have your own marketing message. When you're yelling from the mountaintops how great you are, it makes people want to turn the opposite direction.

I've done business for *years* without a business card.

When people ask how to contact me I say, "Get out your cell phone; I'll give you my number."

Or when they want to look at my website, I'll say, "Let's have a conversation. Looking at a website doesn't really tell you very much. If you're that interested, let's talk."

What I'm doing by not having print marketing is encouraging voice-to-voice conversation. That's the way real business gets done: Talking.

People talking to people.

Stop:
- » Having people click around the internet
- » Sending ads in the mail
- » Handing out flyers
- » Shoving your business cards in people's faces

Instead:
- » Have heart-to-heart conversations
- » Communicate
- » Truly unite with people

DON'T WASTE TIME

If you are sitting in your home or office creating brochures and business cards and logos and websites then you aren't letting people know about you and they aren't getting a taste of you. They are wasting your time and taking you away from relationship building.

Get out and mingle. Here is an idea that will be fun!

What are your hobbies? What are your interests? What are your passions? Go spend time doing what you love with people who also love doing that.

In my business, I love working out, I love speaking, reading and the ocean. I do my marketing by going to the gym and chatting with people for fun. When they ask, "What do you do?" we chat deeper.

I speak on stages all over the world because I love meeting new people, I write blogs, articles, and books because it is fun for me and I connect with my readers. I hang out at the beach, chat with other people there, and we often talk about what we do in our careers.

See how natural, easy, and effortless this is? Instead of forcing myself to some networking group or chamber meeting, I go do what is fun for me and I meet new people. When people are around other people who are having fun, they are magnetized to them.

CHAPTER TWO - LEAVE THE PAST IN THE PAST

STOP TRYING TO CONVERT PEOPLE

Many salespeople try to influence us, convince us, and tell us how wonderful they are. They have spent their time and energy with intricate sales scripts that were very manipulative. Consumers have a problem because of not being able to say no. They use a lot of psychological practices, and maybe neurolinguistics programming, or neurolinguistics language; so, people buy something they didn't necessarily want because of the sales scripting. Pressure is not a good sales tactic.

Salespeople overcome our every objection, and we have nothing else left. Some people return what they bought, or get angry about what they bought and write a negative review online, or are unhappy with products and services and vow to never buy from the seller again.

You might wonder how I can say this. I say it because the way most people have trained, coached, consulted or mentored people to market is the farthest thing from being a heart-based business owner and repels people from you instead of magnetizing people to you.

Here is a prime example.

I spoke to someone about a texting service he provided. I told him I "might" be interested and to give me a few months to see if we had this need in my business. Right after the call he sent me follow up emails "selling" me on the benefits of his service. Now, I wasn't sure I wanted the service and the last thing I wanted were a bunch of emails.

Wait, there's more! A few weeks later (remember I said to give me a few months), he emailed me and phoned me trying to "sell" his services again. I was now officially turned off and tuned out.

I happened to be at a Polka Dot Powerhouse connection meeting when a woman in the group told about her texting services. I inquired. We spoke by phone and she did no selling. She listened to what I wanted, then explained how her service could provide the benefits I wanted and told me to contact her when and if I was ready. Breath of fresh air!

Here is the funny part. They both represented the exact same company! I am still deciding if I want this service. She has connected with me on Facebook, liking, commenting and sharing my posts. As for the gentleman, he emailed and called me again and this time I said the answer was "no".

Which type of business owner do you choose to be? One who runs after prospects chasing them, begging them to do business with you and tries to convince them to buy from you? Or do you want to be of service, allow people to know you exist, and are happy to serve them? Since you are reading this book I know your answer.

Please forget whatever you have been taught about sales and marketing and let me show you how to attract your ideal prospects who are qualified and excited to receive the benefits and outcomes you provide.

NO MORE SCRIPTED SALES TALK

I used to close sales, and I knew how to overcome objections and use sales scripts. I was actually very good at it. However, I never felt like I worked with integrity. It felt like I played the sales game to sell something customers didn't necessarily want, and maybe I didn't even know if they could use.

Conversion should be a process that:

» Allows buyers—not sellers—to have the upper hand
» Fosters goodwill
» Allows the buyer to convert themselves
» Is an effortless process in which people look at what you have, get excited about it, fall in love with it, and want to buy it

DON'T OVERCOME OBJECTIONS

Using language that tries to close the sale is an obvious attempt to make people buy.

For example:

"Do you want to pay with MasterCard or Visa?" is an obvious push.

People are wise to those kinds of questions. Avoid closing language, because people know they're being closed in on. Buyers are very smart now. They tend to resist.

Also, when you overcome their objections, if you beat them down until they finally have no objection left, then you have not done a good job of helping that person make a buying decision. Most buyers will not feel very good about you as a seller.

If somebody has an objection, allow the person to have it.

If they think that the price is too high, you don't have to convince them that they're looking at it the wrong way. The price is high! They can decide to buy it or not buy it. If they are not sure they like this color red, you don't have to tell them this is the most beautiful color red and how great it looks on them.

You can say, "Decide if you want it."

Do not get involved in overcoming their objections. Let them make their choice, and when they come from a place of choice, they'll buy, and sales will stick.

When you don't have to worry about overcoming objections, you can stay present with the person that you're communicating with. You can focus on their wants and their needs, and can let go of any thoughts about what the outcome is going to be. You're not trying to gain anything or win anything, you're just two people in a conversation so that the other person gets to make a decision. That's the way a sale should go.

DON'T USE CONVINCING MARKETING

Convincing marketing is a situation in which you want to create a reaction in someone to buy. You want to control the outcome. In convincing marketing, what we're doing is spending a lot of time and energy talking about ourselves, talking about how great our business or company is.

The message of convincing marketing is, "Hey, my stuff is amazing! You should buy it. You need it."

This is the worst approach that you could have, especially these days when people don't want to hear about how awesome you are or that you're some kind of guru. You don't need to convince them of that. Nobody wants to buy from those people. In fact, the guru-centric model does not instill confidence in buyers.

Buyers are becoming increasingly confident. Being a guru does not endear you to a buyer. What's much more important is to use your marketing to get people to raise their hands. Allow them to feel the magnetic pull to you. Then you don't spend any time or energy convincing them of anything. That's not your job.

When you use convincing marketing, you know when you have caused a reaction in a buyer. I encourage you not to feel good about that. When you convince someone to do something, and they have not convinced themselves, that's when you will most likely get returns. You probably won't get that person as a long-term customer. That person may not ever refer anyone else to you.

CHAPTER TWO - LEAVE THE PAST IN THE PAST

Never feel good or ethical in trying to convince someone to do, be, or buy something that you have.

What's so beautiful about giving up on converting people is that there are so many easy, effortless ways to magnetize people right to you. There are ways to put yourself in front of the people who already want what you're providing, and to allow them to raise their hand. Once they raise their hand, then you encourage them to make their own buying decision.

It takes all the pressure off you; it lets you speak just to your ideal target audience, and because you can do that now so easily with social media like Facebook, Twitter, and LinkedIn, your ideal target audience can make a very quick decision to purchase.

You do not have to scream from the rooftops; customers will find you.

They will say, "I want what you have. How do I buy it?"

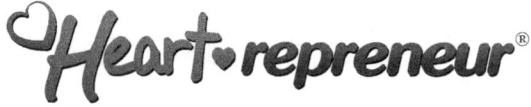

WHAT TERRI GIVES YOU FREE

As a fellow Heart-repreneur® you can watch Terri's training webinar anytime you want to learn how to create your high-ticket signature program and get an automated flow of qualified leads to contact you. https://www.heart-repreneur.com/master-class

You can read Terri's latest business articles designed to keep you turbocharged. https://heartrepreneur.com/blog/

Schedule a call with the Heart-repreneur® team to see if you are a good fit for Terri to help you.

https://www.heart-repreneur.com/new-strategy-session-page

Grab the free course I just put together for you so you can get tons of qualified prospects fast: https://gethotpayingclients.com/

You can listen to Heart-repeneur® Radio and hear interviews that will give you a lot of tips and tools to help you in your business and your life https://itunes.apple.com/us/podcast/heartrepreneur-radio/id1159942743?mt=2

Download past episodes or subscribe to future episodes of Heart-repreneur® Radio by Terri Levine for free.

You can tune in to Terri TV and get business advice from Terri and her guest experts and co-hosts at www.terri.tv

Get thousands of dollars of free courses and trainings when you set up a free account at https://www.heartrepreneuracademy.com/

CHAPTER TWO - LEAVE THE PAST IN THE PAST

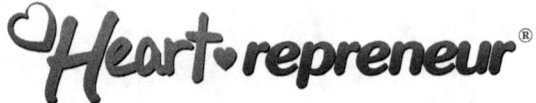

Join the Heart-repreneur® Movement here today:

Join our community at https://www.facebook.com/groups/heart-repreneurswithterrilevine and help us transform how business is done and shift your own business to a conscious business. You are reading this book because you want to be doing business cooperatively and to maximize relationships.

CHAPTER THREE

MAKE IT FUN, EASY, AND EFFORTLESS

CHAPTER THREE - MAKE IT FUN, EASY, AND EFFORTLESS

SET UP FREEDOM SYSTEMS

Many people get into business because they want to have more freedom. They don't want a *job*. They get into business but they don't have the right systems that free up their time and lives. Their businesses become and feel the same as a job. They feel stuck.

They're trapped under a lot of email, paperwork, and a lot of firefighting. They really feel like their business is sucking up their time and energy, and they don't have freedom to pursue their goals outside of their business.

Many people don't even remember what their goals are! It's very important to understand that you can be free in your own business. You can get a lot more done in an efficient way, in a lot less time, when you've created systems that make your business run like a very well-oiled machine.

That's why you need freedom systems in all areas of your business:

» Hiring
» Training
» Cultivating teamwork
» Customer satisfaction

- Managing finances
- Marketing
- Operations
- Leadership

Freedom systems create entrepreneurs who are happy in their businesses.

KNOW YOUR BRILLIANCE

People think when they are the owner they need to do everything. So very often, they're the one who's doing. In fact, they're so busy "doing," they can't work on their business. Michael Gerber talks about this in his book, *The E-Myth*, and I found this to be true in my own business.

When I first started, I was doing everything. I was a speech-language pathologist. I worked with patients, did the marketing, scheduling, collections, and managing the team as well.

I wasn't doing anything very well because I was trying to do everything. I learned that if I focused on the things that only I could do using my unique talents, easily and effortlessly, then the company could advance a lot further.

I teach this to solopreneurs. Once they get this in place, and they're *only* working with their strengths and talents (their brilliance), their companies make more money, and the business owners are happier.

Something is not an area of your brilliance if it feels:

- Difficult
- Not enjoyable
- Like a struggle

That's when you're going to find that you're overworking. That's when your work-life balance feels off.

DELEGATE, DELEGATE, DELEGATE

List the things that you're not brilliant at. What tasks feel more like a chore?

What makes you feel stuck and takes away your feeling of independence?

Then find people who can easily and effortlessly do those things for you.

For core competency, you want to make sure that you're delegating so that other people get to do the work that you don't enjoy or that you're not the most talented to do. It gives you time to focus only on your brilliance. It will increase your revenues and profits, just the way it has for me and for my clients.

INSTRUCTIONS FACILITATE AUTOMATION

Whatever needs to be done in your business, you want systems. From the systems, you want to create automation.

Whatever needs to be done, whether you're doing it or whether you've delegated it, make sure that the process is written down in great detail and as a matter of fact.

For example, say you own a gym and every day the treadmills needed to be oiled, wiped down, and the belts checked. You consult a written system manual that would tell you who is going to do it, when they're going to do it, and how they're going to do it. The schedule and instructions should be written so a fifth-grader could read them, pick up the task, and do it.

This allows you to create a replicable system that's not dependent upon specific people. If you leave, someone else can pick up the instructions, read them, and that very day they can take charge of the system you've put in place.

When you do this, you'll find that you are able to have more free time.

You'll also be in a better position to sell the business, if you want to, at some future point.

The reason that you want to have freedom systems is to create work-life balance. Your business shouldn't become a boring chore. You want to own your business, not be owned by it.

Put systems and automation in place so your business can:

- » Grow
- » Give you independence
- » Create more free time
- » Generate more money

This will truly allow you to get more value out of each task or issue at work and enjoy what you're doing outside of work.

LEVERAGE AND AUTOMATE EVERYTHING

In order to create your business so it does not feel like a job, things need to run like a well-oiled machine without you.

Is it possible to do this without having as many employees or independent contractors?

A business is nothing more than a set of systems. Once you have these systems in place, you're going to find that your entire business functions better and the systems allow you to create more income in less time.

When you set up your business this way:

» There aren't bottlenecks.
» Cash can come in more easily and effortlessly.
» People are hired and trained without headaches.
» You can make sure you have the right people.
» Teamwork is smooth.

Even your customers can communicate with you easily and effortlessly.

USE EVERYTHING IN THREE TO FIVE WAYS

When you do something, you don't want to have to repeat it. First you design a system, whether you're creating a webinar or a book. Whatever you're creating, think about how you can move from doing it once, to making it work in another three to five ways.

Here's how you can leverage a single event. As an example, I'll use the webinar I did last week.

1. **Take the action once.** Then I made the recording of that webinar available, so that people who couldn't make it can come to my website and watch it.
2. **Transcribe the recorded event.** The second thing that I did to leverage it was to have transcriptions done from the webinar, so that people who don't want to sit and watch the whole webinar can download it into an e-report and read all or part of it.
3. **Create an audio file.** The third way I leveraged it was I had the audio extracted, so that people who prefer to listen can do so.
4. **Make videos widely available.** To take things even further, the next thing I did was upload it to YouTube.
5. **Use excerpts on social media.** I took it even further—from the transcription, we're now using pieces of that for my Tweets and for Facebook. We're going to take a section and use it for three to five blog posts.

So, you take the action once, and you use it multiple ways. That's how you free up your time.

ALLOW AUTOMATION TO HELP YOU

Many times, people resist automated things. They're almost afraid to turn things over to an automated system. For example, some of my clients felt like they had to go onto Facebook, Twitter or LinkedIn daily to connect with social media contacts, until I had them keep a journal, recording where they spend every fifteen minutes of their day for two weeks.

They realized how much time they were using to check social media, and that they could be using their free time instead to be with friends, or with family, or to market their business, or to do something productive.

Automation is out there. It's not very expensive, and it can work for *all* areas of your business, including managing finances, training people, motivating people who work with you, having your team connect on projects, or making sure your customers are wowed.

Any area of business systems can not only be simplified, but multiplied. So, when something gets done, it becomes a process to automate. Automation, leveraging, and optimizing create profitable systems.

FREE YOUR TIME FOR MONEYMAKING ACTIVITIES

A business owner always needs to be marketing their business. In my view, that's the most important job you have as a business owner. If you're not bringing in new prospects and new customers to the business, then you're not going to be in business for very long. So, you must have time on your calendar—a significant amount of it—each week, every single week, to work on your business and especially market your business.

Many business owners don't create this kind of time, and when they don't create this time, then they're not able to bring in more customers, and the business suffers. In addition, they're not able to focus on their current and past customers being wowed. If people aren't wowed, they won't stay long term, and they won't have any brand loyalty. Customers will leave as soon as somebody less expensive is pointed out to them.

The biggest message that an entrepreneur can hear are the two words *leverage* and *optimize*.

In order to:

» Be successful in business long term
» Really enjoy your business long term
» Have a profitable business long term

You have to have a business that is leveraged and optimized.

It's really not a choice. It's a HAVE to. *You have to do this.* If you don't have leverage, you'll be working very long hours in your business.

Working long hours leads to:

» Stress
» Anxiety
» Burnout

Working long hours does not lead to creativity, which you need as a business owner.

If your business is not optimized, leveraged, and automated, you do things over and over again, which is very costly.

You'll never have the kind of bottom line you desire, which can lead not only to the same frustrations, but also cause you to go out of business.

Optimize and Leverage. Don't forget them.

CHAPTER THREE - MAKE IT FUN, EASY, AND EFFORTLESS

THE RIGHT PEOPLE CONVERT THEMSELVES

Business owners work way too hard at trying to attract the most interested audience. Typically, their message is going out to a large group—not their ideal, exact, specific client group—and because of that, they spend a lot of time, money, and energy hunting for people who can show up and be their clients, or their customers, or patients.

As a business owner, I know that this can easily put a business under.

Business owners must know the exact way to attract their ideal—and *only* their ideal, hoped for targets, who raise their hands to say, "I want in! Here's my check, credit card or cash."

It's easy to target your audience. It takes a lot less time, energy, and money to sell just to them. You'll get to help the people who really need and want what you provide.

GET THE MESSAGE TO THE RIGHT SEGMENT OF THE MARKET

When you've truthfully identified your exact, specific target audience, all you'll want to do is spend your marketing time positioning your message so that they get to hear it. We want your message, what I call a *Core Unique Positioning Statement*, to show up in front of the people who already have a need for your product or service. They're already raising their hand. They're already searching, speaking, or looking for what you have.

All you need to do is get the message right in front of them. You don't need to sell to them; you don't need to work hard. All you need to do is present yourself and make your message noticeable.

Get your message to your very specific, targeted audience. That message will create a magnet.

Your ideal, target audience will be magnetized to:

» Follow you
» Come to you
» Call you
» Go to your store
» Buy from you

They will see your message, and they will want to take action on your message. You will not have to convince people anymore.

WHOM CAN YOU HELP RIGHT NOW?

Think about what kind of help you can give people, and the results that you can give people quickly.

You're not hunting for anybody.

You're attracting people who:

» Already have a need
» Already have an interest
» Are going to take action

It's important that you're focusing only on the right people. That's why you've got to have clarity in your message. You don't want to attract people who don't fit, because during the process where they're converting themselves, you may end up with clients, patients, or customers who don't fit. They will end up costing you a lot of money, energy, or time.

If you get your marketing message across to people who don't fit or don't resonate with the message, you're going to find that you're wasting a lot of time, and that these people don't convert easily.

So, you want to hone in on not only the specific target audience, but also a target audience who is perfect for what you're advertising. Not only do they want and need what you have, but they're also the kind of people to whom you would like to provide your products and services.

You also want to be sure that you can immediately help them fulfill their need. You don't want to have prospects that sit on a list, that you have to keep parading in front of to get your message to them. That takes a lot of energy and time, and it doesn't generate income for your business right now.

You want to get in front of people right here, today, right now; but you also want your prospects to be looking for services right in the moment.

For example, let's say I'm having really bad allergies and I want relief. I'm watching a commercial, or reading a newspaper or magazine, or talking with a friend, or scrolling through social media—wherever I may look—I'm on the lookout for a solution. If the solution shows up through one of those venues, I want to purchase it immediately. I'm a perfect fit for the product.

You want to be sure as the seller that you can help people right now. You're looking to connect through your media messages with people who want to purchase your services or products right now. Position your message so people who need your product or service right now can see it.

CEMENT THE MARKET

You can take a whole different market if you show people specifically that you:

- » Know what they're looking for
- » Have the answers they're looking for
- » Understand their pain
- » Can give them results through your products or services

That is what you need to provide people. That is what they truly want to buy *right now*.

Conversion happens automatically when people already see and resonate with your Core Unique Positioning Statement, and they see the intrinsic value that you bring. They will be excited to buy your products and services because they already feel an affinity for you.

You want to be able to attract people and instantly show them the benefits and value they will experience after purchasing your products or services. In your messaging and in your closing process or conversion process with your target audience, you want to make sure that you can provide examples from past customers who can show fast results.

Past customers who experience success will refer people to you, and they'll be thrilled to continue to buy from you or stay with you long term.

Anyone who experienced waiting a long time for a result from your company, your product, or your service is not an ideal customer or client.

WORK WITH ONLY THE BEST

Often a business will create sales because they need revenue, and they don't really care about the business. They're happy to make a sale and see that as a way to achieve their revenue goals.

Unfortunately, this takes a toll on businesses. I work with a lot of clients that have had very poor experiences by taking in less-than-ideal customers, patients, or clients. Those clients or customers become energy vampires.

They may:

- » Become complainers
- » Demand chargebacks
- » Take their rants to social media

You want to be very cautious about those with whom you do business. You need to have some very good criteria and guidelines with whom you choose to work with. You're allowed to be picky.

A couple years ago, there was a client about whom I didn't have great feelings, and something in my gut told me not to take him on, but I did. This client took so much energy and eventually so much time from my consulting team that his project cost us about ten times more than he paid.

He sent emails saying how wonderful we were doing and how he benefited from the project. The project was completed, and at the time, he was happy. But several months later, around Christmas time, he wanted all his money back.

None of this was his fault. It was my fault, as a business owner, for accepting just anyone into the business.

Be protective, and your business will be stable and secure.

The best people—the ones who are ideal, targeted, just right, and have fitting personalities and attitudes—will be your raving fans. They will not only stay with you for the long run and keep buying from you, they will shout from the rooftops how great your products and services are. These are the *only* kinds of people you want to do business with.

One more thing: You magnetize the right people to you or your business, because you didn't spend energy or time selling them anything. They are the ones to decide if they want to purchase, what they want to purchase, and to make the purchase. They're willing, they're ready, and all they need to do is see that you can help them, that you're ready to help them with your product or service, and they will actually close the sale themselves. There is a lot less drain and strain on your business when you work with these partners.

ALWAYS BE MARKETING

Did you know that the quantity of direct mail doubled over the past decade? That's right. The average household receives twice as much direct mail today as it did 10 years ago. And on average you receive about 3,000 marketing messages per day.

People are sick and tired of hype and advertising. They are surrounded by lots of companies who seem to offer the same thing and have many choices.

Did you also know that 95% of businesses fail in ten years? You might be one of those! I wrote the original edition of *Turbocharge* and then created this revised edition to help you survive and actually turbocharge your business, just like I do for my clients every day.

I know you want to have fun in business while contributing to society and making a difference for others. That's not to say you don't enjoy money. You deserve to be paid well for what you provide for others.

If you aren't marketing regularly in an ethical and authentic way then you are selfishly keeping your gifts from others and you may be one of the 95% who is out of business. I believe you have something of value to offer and I want you to be able to provide that. If people don't know about you and what you offer then people can't buy from you and soon you will disappear as a business entity.

People discover products and services through marketing.

I want to see your business thrive not just survive and this is why you need to be marketing all the time in an authentic and conscious way. Consumers are more conscious today. They do business with companies

CHAPTER THREE - MAKE IT FUN, EASY, AND EFFORTLESS

they trust and look for transparency and authenticity and accountability.

You want to be a business that is not only a conscious business you also want to be able to market and to grow and promote your business in a way that's in alignment with your integrity.

Forget high pressure sales, "closing techniques", overcoming objections and all forms of slick marketing. Marketing is focusing on spreading your word and is based on creating relationships with people.

When I say always be marketing I mean consciously attract people to you that you want to serve with your products and services.

CONSCIOUSLY GROW YOUR BUSINESS

To consciously grow your business you must be authentic, honest, transparent, committed to long term relationships and not quick sales, focused on your local market and interested in attracting and not chasing after qualified prospects.

I call this reverse marketing. This means you market your products and services and people come to you instead of you chasing after them.

There is no need to sell. Just allow people to be drawn to what you offer and to make their own decisions. You don't have to promote and sell to people any more. Reverse selling by attraction is what is needed to turbocharge your business.

How do you do this? You must look at your business and think about how your business can be more attractive to your target audience. You must remove any pressure or expectations so that you can turbocharge your business. Pressure and expectations repel people and authenticity and honesty attract people.

Commit to being totally honest and transparent. Be your word. You are your word and nothing but your word in business and in life.

I talk to people every day. I simply build a relationship based on trust and I create a safe space for us to build from. I never focus on closing anyone. I simply engage in conversations and create value. I don't even follow up with people. I share what I have and what I can do for them and allow them to either resonate and make a decision or not.

Marketing is having conversations and building relationships that are natural, that we enjoy, and feel good about. The marketing you do is based on what feels good to you.

You need to have a few things in place to successfully market your business. First, you need a clear and specific niche. This is the market you wish to target.

You also want to have an offering for the niche that is based upon outcomes they have told you they want.

Then, you need to know where to find the people in the niche to make your offering to, and once you find them, you must have a way to build trust with them.

Let's use one of my clients to illustrate how she made the shift from marketing to people to reverse marketing where people are attracted to her.

We began her consulting with a deep understanding and identification of her niche. We discovered what they really wanted. Instead of focusing on finding her niche one person at a time we located an ideal target market of qualified prospects who shared her hobbies, interests and passions and that she could relate to. She is a Naturopathic Doctor and we found groups that had like-minded people into health and wellness, natural healing, Reiki, acupuncture and massage.

We found a community group for her to be a part of and she began to cater her business to this group and their values. She got known for working with other holistic healthcare providers as their Naturopathic Doctor by being part of this crowd. So, we physically located her audience and now we had to have the right message for them.

We put together her Core Unique Positioning Statement so she could tell people in all her online and offline marketing this statement, "I help alternative health care practitioners and their clients who are dealing

CHAPTER THREE - MAKE IT FUN, EASY, AND EFFORTLESS

with health issues and want to find a natural way to allow their bodies to heal themselves."

The final thing she had to do was to create a very attractive offer that her qualified prospects would like to take her up on. I had her ask her prospects what they would like her to offer. Most people create an offer and then hope their ideal target audience is interested enough to respond to their offer.

Instead, I had her find out what offer would be totally irresistible for her niche. Based on their responses she created a Natural Living Assessment that they could take and submit to her and then receive a consult with her to create their Natural Living Plan.

Once her business started to take off I taught her to do stay in touch marketing. This is easy. She invited people to local seminars and to teleseminars where she taught valuable educational, content. She dropped people notes and cards regularly using Send Out Cards (https://www.sendoutcards.com/104581).

She began to be seen as a trusted advisor that people wanted to come to and were attracted to instead of marketing to them. She was building relationships, keeping top of mind and doing business heart to heart through connection. I had her focus on doing business in this way.

Jay Abraham, one of my mentors, taught me that there are only 3 ways to grow a business. You can get more customers, you can sell higher priced items to those customers or you can have them come back more often and make repeat purchases. Most business owners spend almost all their time trying to get more customers.

That is, in my experience, why 95% will go out of business. Instead of my client focusing on more customers, once we got the ball rolling and clients in the door, the entire focus became encouraging her client family to come in more often. She also provided some packages that were a bit more expensive and were jammed packed with value. She spent time giving her client family special offers with more and more value and having fun serving them. That's how we turbocharge a business!

Today, I have her focusing on her top family members who give her 80% of her business. She gives them special attention. She offers all her family members gifts, too. She gives them coupons they can pass on to their friends and family and their own patients (if they own a business treating patients), to receive a free Natural Wellness Assessment and Consult with her.

When the people they refer use the coupons she then gives them a very special discounted offer because they were referred by a family member. She also thanks the client family member for the referral and gives them a gift as well.

FREE EVENTS EDUCATE AND INSPIRE

I strongly believe all business owners should invite qualified prospects to community educational events that they host. Let me show you this in action with another client example:

My client offers weight loss shakes and supplements through a direct sales company. Each month she hosts a "Shake And Mix" event. She invites all her prospects and clients to attend a get together where she shares her shakes and other products. She doesn't pitch her products or the direct marketing business opportunity.

People mix, mingle, and chat. She answers their questions and has a 47% conversion ratio, which is awesome. People are connected, having fun, and are attracted to her shakes. Because they have just spent time with her, she has mixed with them, and answered their questions, many of them are ready to use her products.

People in her community are raving about these events and anxious to attend each month. She gives away free passes for her next event to all of those attending, to all current family members, and asks people to invite their friends to come next month.

COMMUNITY IS KEY

I have built communities online for my clients that are closed Facebook groups that only they can access. In addition, I have built about 10 Facebook groups that serve the different types of qualified prospects that want the results I deliver with my programs and those are open to everyone.

(https://www.facebook.com/groups/heartrepreneurswithterrilevine).

Why build these Facebook communities? The ones for my clients are a no-brainer. They interact with each other. They connect and help each other. Plus, I am there giving them more coaching, tools and resources. If there is a new event, program or service I want to let them know about it, is easy for me to connect and I don't have to worry that my emails might not get through. Facebook sends notifications to people who are part of groups.

For my non-client groups, this is how I bring qualified prospects into my world. I provide value, education, content in my posts, and with Facebook Live. Word of mouth of my Facebook communities spreads. People invite their friends and others. The momentum leads to a group of people who are interested in getting to know me, like me and may come to trust me as I deliver value and outcomes for them.

Maybe they aren't ready to spend 10 minutes with me on the phone yet. They can, however, hang out in my group. What can you do with your Facebook group? You can have discussions, talk about issues, give away resources and tools, give support, check in and see how people are doing. Assign homework, have people send their homework through the group, share documents or simply ask what they need or want help with. I even run challenges in some of my groups like this one:

https://www.facebook.com/groups/10kin45minutes .

People who have been part of that challenge have later entered my programs if it resonated with them.

By having Facebook groups where I participate and converse with my clients and prospects I am giving people value and allowing them to try me on deeper and to go further with me.

CHAPTER THREE - MAKE IT FUN, EASY, AND EFFORTLESS

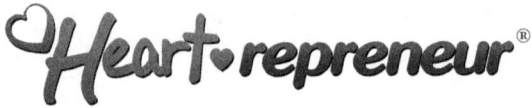

DID YOU KNOW THE HEART-REPRENEUR® TEAM WILL GIVE YOU PERSONAL ADVICE?

As a reader and fellow Heart-repreneur® you can schedule a phone consult with our team. This session is your Turbocharge business game plan. We will go very deep into your business and sort out and solve your business problems. We will expose any overlooked problems and use Terri›s decades of experience to share tools, tips and strategies with you.

Your session will deep dive anything and everything related to your business and can include: lead generation, your online and offline sales process, increasing conversions without selling, your business model, marketing tactics, business operations and anything else business related you choose.

This is a very focused session customized and designed so you walk away with a game plan to fix what isn't quite yet right in your business and will set you up for a great future from a highly regarded business growth strategist who does business as a Heart-repreneur®.

Because you are a reader of this book you can schedule your session now.

If you are serious about turbocharging your business and want Terri's help as someone who has guided the success of over 5,000 other business owners, entrepreneurs and marketers for many decades and believe her real-world experience and Heart-repreneur® style can help you grow your business then grab this opportunity to get a personal consult. This session is yours to ask specific questions, to pick our brains and get advice, information, and knowledge to help you grow your business.

https://www.heart-repreneur.com/new-strategy-session-page

CHAPTER FOUR

• • • • • • • • • •

SHOW AND TELL

GIVE PEOPLE PRACTICAL VALUE

There are a lot of people who are probably looking for your products and services. It's really important to position your business and yourself as willing to give away, to share, and to be open-hearted. You can magnetize more people this way. Not only do you need the right positioning, but you also need to provide value.

Value actually affects your price, how people perceive you, and your bottom line. So, it's very important that you look at the value of what you bring from a practical standpoint and from an intrinsic standpoint. When you add those two together, you're going to attract people easily and effortlessly. People will be willing to pay you for your products and services at the price that you've established.

GIVE AWAY YOUR BEST SERVICES OR PRODUCTS

Allow people to sample a product or service you offer that is of true value to them:

- » If you're a massage therapist, maybe you give them a sample massage.
- » If you're a chiropractor, maybe you give them a small treatment.

- » If you're a business consultant, maybe you give them a little bit of consulting.
- » If you're a life coach, maybe you give them a little bit of life coaching.
- » If you're a florist, maybe you put a sign out advertising that on Tuesdays, every customer whose first names starts with a "B" can get a free rose.

The idea here is to allow people to surface from under the iceberg where they've been hiding. These are the people who don't want to be known.

They just peek their heads out a little bit and say, "Oh, that looks interesting. Let me try it on with no obligations, with no fear that somebody is going to sell me anything or pitch me anything. Let me raise my hand and say to you, 'I might be your target audience, but I'm not sure yet. I would like to try you on since there's no obligation.'"

If they're the right clients, when they try you or your products on, they will find them highly valuable. Chances are they're going to want more. So, the best thing you can do is be fearless.

Give your best products, services, and information with no fear at all, from a loving and generous heart.

DEMONSTRATE WHAT YOU'RE ABLE TO DO

You want to be able to demonstrate exactly what you're able to do, so that people understand the true benefits of purchasing from your company, engaging in your services, or using your products.

What are the true benefits you offer?

You could *tell* people the benefits, but when you tell people, it truly sounds like you're selling.

For example, you may have visited a wonderful home that you're

CHAPTER FOUR - SHOW AND TELL

thinking of purchasing, but I want you to buy my house instead. So, I keep telling you about how wonderful my home is, what its great qualities are, and why my home is the right home for you. Rather than make you want to buy my house, it might make you want to back up and walk away.

This happened to me recently. I went into a store and I tried on a very expensive leather jacket. It was beautiful and I was 80 percent sure I was going to purchase it.

Then a salesperson came over and said, "Oh, this looks great on you! It's the right size for you. Nobody looks as good in this color as you do! It's great with your hair, it's great with your eye color!"

She kept pushing and pushing. In a few minutes, all I wanted to do was run away. I left the store without the jacket—the jacket that I was going to buy.

When I got in the car I asked myself: *Why am I leaving without the jacket?*

I was just about ready to take out my credit card. I had justified the expense (which was a little bit ridiculous).

Why am I leaving without it?

I realized it was because somebody was throwing-up benefits all over me.

Being pushy turns potential customers off.

Instead, when you give something that is truly great and beneficial and helpful, you want *the recipient* to recognize the benefit. They will see the intrinsic value. They'll come to their own realization that your product or service is giving them a better result.

It could be a better result in your client's:

» Health
» Business
» Relationship

» Energy

Or in whatever area your services and products address.

When you let prospects taste your product, when you let them try you on and you give them something that is truly valuable, they will know the benefits and you don't have to sell them.

DON'T BE ATTACHED TO THE OUTCOME

When you offer a taste test or a free pass, try not to predict the result.

You may be tempted to think: *Oh, good, now I have them. Now they're going to buy from me.*

In truth, you don't want to be attached at all, because if you're attached, you're getting into the sales mentality of wanting to hook the customer.

Instead:

» Put your goods out there in the universe.
» Allow people to try them on.
» Allow people to magnetically come to you.
» Allow them to raise their hands.

I worked with a client who helps people to become better athletes. He ran a one-day sports camp on a Saturday. People could join the camp with no obligation. About forty or fifty people came. He ran the sports camp as if they were high-paying clients; he gave them all the value that he typically gives. He had zero attachment to whether any of them were going to sign up for his program.

Zero.

He just did it for the sake of doing it, giving for the sake of giving, and the right people raised their hands and inquired.

CHAPTER FOUR - SHOW AND TELL

He didn't do a pitch. He didn't make an ad.

He didn't do a commercial. He didn't try to sell.

The right people asked:

"Hey, how can we do this again?" "Do you do this often?"

"Do you do this regularly?"

He didn't even have a pitch prepared.

He said, "I don't have anything prepared; I'm not even prepared to tell you how this normally works."

They kept asking.

Finally, he said, "At the end of the day I'll sit down with those of you who are interested and I'll tell you a little bit about it. If you want to do it, do it; and if not, we'll part as friends."

He reported to me that thirteen people stayed to sit in the little group, and of those, six signed up. He didn't make an offer to them; they just handed over their credit cards. A few days later, four more signed up to say they wanted to do it again.

I can honestly tell you, he had no intention of selling, no attachment to the outcome, and that's why he was successful.

KNOW THE QUESTIONS YOUR PROSPECTS ASK, AND ANSWER THEM

What are your prospects dealing with?

What are their problems?

What are their situations?

What's happening in the marketplace?

What are they concerned or confused about?

What kind of questions might they have before buying your products or services?

What do they need to know?

What holds them back from moving forward using your products and services?

Every time someone is thinking of making a purchasing decision, they have questions in their mind about the purchase.

Thinking back to the example of when I wanted to buy the expensive jacket, I was asking myself:

What leather is this?

Is this going to hold up for a long time?

It's very expensive. Should I spend this kind of money?

Does it look good on me? Does it fit me well? Is it the right color?

Anytime someone is making a purchasing decision, you want to understand what they're thinking. The most important thing that they're thinking about has to do with making a purchase that is going to give the results that they want.

If the customers don't believe psychologically that your product or service is going to aid in their life or in their work, and be worth the dollars that they're spending, they're not going to want to do business with you.

People who are ready to make a purchase have questions in their minds. You want to think of what the questions might be, and begin to answer the questions before they are asked. I've done this recently by launching several videos where I simply answer questions before people ask them. I'm talking about the things that you might think about before you're making a purchase.

You might do a consumer awareness guide.

For example: *Things to Be Aware of Before You Hire a Contractor.*

Again, think of what your audience is concerned about, and answer their questions first, before they ask them of you.

GROUND THE PRACTICAL VALUE FIRST

There's a lot of value that you can offer people. Practical value is something that everybody relates to. It's something that people need to know in order to make an informed buying decision. If I'm going to spend a lot of money on the jacket I've been talking about, first I must understand the practical value. I must ask myself:

Is this made well?

Is this going to last?

Then, once I really understand the practical value, the intrinsic value sets the price.

Intrinsic value is the unseen value that's created when we do positioning and promotion. Intrinsic values are the feel-good kinds of things. Intrinsic value is why you're willing to pay more for a BMW than you are for a Prius. They're both cars, they're both practical, they both drive, but there's intrinsic value in owning something different and special.

You must have practical value so that people are willing to invest in intrinsic value. Make sure you ground the practical value first.

POSITIONING THAT'S MYSTERIOUS AND EXCITING

When you're positioning your message, there are many ways to do it, and to make your company, your products, your services, or yourself appear in a certain way. All of this is called *pre-framing*. It's how people think about you before they even purchase from you. In your positioning, you want to seek people's attention. You want to keep their interest.

You also want to establish what your marketplace thinks about you or your company. So, as you position, you want to position in a way that has your target audience very, very curious; very, very interested.

You want your audience trying to figure out: "Hmm, who is this company?"

"What is this company?"

Then what you're doing is helping your target audience get more attracted and more magnetized to who you are and what you do.

With pre-framing, you can position yourself or your company as an authority.

Consumers will ask: "What is this?"

"Who is this mysterious person or this very interesting company?"

They will wonder: *Why do I want to know more?*

Consumers will get attracted to knowing more because you will have sparked their curiosity. Sometimes, you don't even have to give details. I have a client who just did some webinars last week to promote a book, and did not include much detail at all. The promotional material only said it was a free webinar that would help you learn to count the blessings in your life. It magnetized people and peaked their curiosity.

They asked themselves:

What does that mean, count my blessings?

What is this? Could it be meditation or something?

My client had a lot of people show up because curiosity and mystery is attractive and magnetizes people.

KNOW YOUR MAGIC POWERS

Every company does things differently. It's a part of their core unique position. You're different. You want your marketplace to think differently about you, your products, and your services. You want your prospects to be delighted, and want to do business with you, without selling.

It takes just a little bit of time for you to answer these questions: How would you like your prospects to be attracted to you?

How would you like them to understand your magic—what I call your *magical powers*?

How are you different from everybody else?

The first thing you need to do in establishing a Core Unique Positioning is to discover what makes you, your business, or your company really special—really magical.

- » Maybe you're amazing at cutting curly hair.
- » Maybe you're amazing at helping people figure out their personality type, and then use that in a great way in business.
- » Maybe you're great at helping people make videos that go viral.

Whatever it is, how do you want the marketplace to know you or your company?

Be very specific so that people know exactly what you do and can demand you more.

One magical power is knowing what you stand for—as a business or as a person—and what you stand against. I've been very vocal in the coaching industry for the last ten years about credentialing in the industry and how it's done. It's partly because of some qualities I have.

You can cultivate these qualities as well:

» Strive to be grounded in who you are.
» Do not be afraid to speak your truth.
» Create the magic that causes the right people to gather around you.

Know what you stand for, and whatever it is you stand for, speak about it loudly.

You want to keep that position, whether as an individual or a company, and ask yourself:

What is my Core Unique Positioning?

What am I going to be famous for?

What am I going to be sought-after for?

What do I stand for?

What do I stand against?

Don't be afraid to say what your Core Unique Positioning is. Once you know your Core Unique Positioning, you can frame all your advertising around your magical powers.

FRAME WHAT YOU'RE FAMOUS FOR

It's important that you understand that *you create your own positioning*. The market doesn't create your positioning: You do! You decide what your marketplace is going to think about you. You get to deploy your position.

You get to figure out:

"How do I want to be viewed in the world as a business or a company?"

Then, using your superpowers, you get to stand up and make a claim about who you are and what you do. You get to deploy your position through your Core Unique Positioning Statement.

When you know your magical power, the next step is to make yourself famous for that. You're going to become a celebrity or an authority in the minds of your prospects.

You can tell people what you're famous for. For example, I'm famous for being anti-International Coach Federation credentials and I took a stand in the coaching industry, being one of the first people to boldly speak against the norm.

One company I work with sells ice cream. They became famous for the fun that they have manufacturing the ice cream, the way the employees work together, and the culture they've created.

So, take whatever it is you've created as your magical power, and then put it out there so that people can see how you're different. Now you can show them your fame and notoriety, because you've owned it in your Core Unique Positioning. You've figured out your magical powers. You've claimed, in your Core Unique Positioning, how you're different, and how you're attractive to other people.

My experience has been that income is in direct proportion to how magical you sound, and in direct proportion to how you claim the differences and distinctions, and allowing people to get so excited about the intrinsic value.

What makes up intrinsic value?

» Magic
» Difference

» Positioning

» Celebrity

These are all elements of your creation.

When you create intrinsic value, it becomes very simple for people to resonate with your awesomeness, to raise their hand and say, "I like you. I want to purchase your products or services."

It's creating value by positioning, by pre-framing.

You absolutely have allowed people to try you on. You've absolutely given them tremendous value. Now you have to magnetize them.

Without selling, very simply let people know your claim: who you are, what you do, so that people begin to trust you. As you indoctrinate people, they trust you more and more. When they trust you, they want what you have.

Think about this: If you've given a lot of value, if you stake your claim and are not afraid to show your magic, prospects know exactly who you are, what you believe, what you stand for, and what you stand against. They're either going to raise a hand and say, "I'm in," or they're going to run and say, "I don't want what you have. I don't like you. I'm out."

Everything that you've done so far in the process has established trust, and has allowed people to say, "I like what you have, who you are, or what your products and services do."

Once they feel this way, they know you, they like you, they trust you, they're going to want what you have. This is the way that you, without selling, magnetize people to come into your experience, raise their hands, and make a purchase.

BUILD INTRINSIC VALUE

I've given you a lot of information about building more and more value. When you build more value, you get to charge more, and you get to have your target audience appreciate you, adore you, and continue to want your products and services. Extrinsic value is built by the core benefits people receive.

It's very important that you build intrinsic value, which is characterized by the things that you can't put your hands on. Intrinsic value is what makes a product worth more to the buyer, regardless of its practical value. It's the unseen, perceived value. Once again, it comes by positioning and by promotion.

In my business, for example, many years ago I was offering business coaching for $250 a month, and you got four hours of my time for $250. As I got busier and busier, I knew that I couldn't work with that many clients. I needed to work with fewer, so I made a decision.

I knew I was giving practical value, so I decided to build my intrinsic value; I decided to charge more so I could work with fewer clients and serve just a few people much more deeply.

I went on a quest to learn how to build intrinsic value. Intrinsic value means offering the same service; the same business consulting, for instance. Clients are going to get the same great stuff, nothing's going to change.

All I did was add something that made people think it was even more special. Clients got *less* time, but they got the time *in person* with me versus on the phone. They got to mastermind with me. They got books. They got every product I ever created, 132 products. Those extras allowed me to charge more.

Intrinsic value will allow you to boost your profit more than anything else. Remember, in terms of profitability, price is number one.

INDOCTRINATE BEFORE YOU CONVERT

Before you even allow a sale to close, you should make sure that people have been *indoctrinated*. I don't mean that you're selling to them, I don't mean that you're overly promoting to them; I mean that they fall in love with your products, with your services, and everything you've done. You show not only the intrinsic as well as the extrinsic value, but you also show what you believe in and what you don't believe in.

We've done it in such a way that people are following us. People are getting very interested in who we are and what we're doing. The marketplace we attract is already thinking about us, and through our promotion, we can tell the marketplace a little bit more, and a little bit more. We indoctrinate them so that they are the ones that end up raising their hands.

Indoctrination basically means you are bringing your clients into your world. Whether they've opted in by visiting your web landing page, or signed up for emails; continue to show them how you do things. Let them become a fan of who you are and what you do. You can do this any number of ways.

Give away:

» Demonstrations
» Free samples
» Videos
» Consumer awareness guides

Like we tell all our clients, try any way that's easy and effortless for you. Teleseminars, teleconferences, whatever it is. You want to tell people about you or your company; show them more. Give even more.

What you say is important. Indoctrination is simply making your positioning stand even stronger. Your income is going to be proportional to how you can indoctrinate people

Indoctrination creates trust.

All you're trying to do is make sure people know you, trust you, and like you even more.

Focus on doing the following:

- » Build intrinsic value
- » Pre-frame that value
- » Position that value

Indoctrination builds the value. When you offer more, more, more, don't assume people will be ready immediately to receive it.

PULL, DON'T PUSH

Pulling is using a magnet, attracting people to you.

Pushing is what happened to me with that wonderful jacket that I wanted to get. Once the pushing started, once someone started selling *to* me, I didn't want to purchase anymore.

You want people to come towards you because you've done a good job of pre-framing and positioning and indoctrinating them. When they do come towards you, you want to make sure that you continue to allow them to come to the magnetic pull. You want them to be excited about you, your products, your services, your company, raising their hand for more and more.

Your prospects peeked out from under the iceberg before, but now they're totally out from underneath. You know who they are, they might be in conversation with you, they might have tried on your products or services. They might be coming to your teleseminars, they might be coming in to get their free rose on a regular basis. They're paying attention to you and they're magnetized to you, so they keep coming back.

You've indoctrinated them, they now believe they want to do business with you.

Their brain is saying, "I want to purchase."

You're not even selling them anything. You haven't even offered them anything!

Somebody came up to me at a non-selling event. It wasn't a pitch-fest. I was speaking from the platform.

As I was moving offstage, a woman was waiting at the bottom of the steps and asked me to make a purchase. I said, "Purchase what?"

I hadn't told the audience what I do, what I offer, or what purchasing would look like. I laughed when this woman was so eager to purchase, even though she didn't know what I was selling.

I realized that I had created so much value that I magnetized the buyer. As it turns out, the woman was on my email list and had been receiving a lot of free value from me. Still, I wasn't *trying* to magnetize the buyer. I didn't try to sell anything, yet there she was, ready to buy whatever I might be selling.

It all goes back to the basics:

» Look at your marketplace.
» Know your customers' questions.
» Position yourself and your message.
» Pre-frame your business.
» Indoctrinate your prospects.

You want to build up so much demand through your intrinsic value that you don't even have to worry about advertising or making an offer. The conversion happens as part of the magnetic process, because you've established with your client the credibility and they know, like, and trust you.

When you position yourself, make sure that you really are different and distinct in the marketplace.

So many coaches, physical therapists, consultants, mentors, and internet marketers sound alike.

How can you be truly different in the marketplace?

CHAPTER FOUR - SHOW AND TELL

It all starts with a Core Unique Positioning Statement. Again, know your powers and your magic, and do not be afraid to be completely different than anybody else in the marketplace. You can do that with just a guarantee.

You can do that with a guarantee for:

- » Money
- » Time
- » Satisfaction

Just make sure:

- » You're distinct and different.
- » You're not a cookie-cutter business.
- » You're not afraid to stand out as an individual or a business.

ALLOW PEOPLE TO TRY YOUR BEST, RISK FREE

Many business owners are afraid to give away their very best services, information, and products, because they think if they do that, people won't make purchases. They think people won't buy their best content, information, programs or products, because they've already given them away for free.

In my experience, the opposite happens.

When people are allowed to truly get an experience of who you are and what you do:

» They get excited

» They are intrigued

» They want more

It creates real momentum and interest.

The service or product you're providing will be even more irresistible to people. There are a lot of different ways that you can do this. It doesn't matter which way you give out samples.

What really matters is that you are fearless in giving away your best information, product, or service.

YOUR BEST INFORMATION IN WEBINARS, TELESEMINARS, AND VIDEOS

First, try to understand what the number one question that prospects are asking themselves. Once you understand what that question is, you want to look for a way that you can provide the answer to the question for free. Again, people will be magnetized to try a sample.

Let's say that you sell Jacuzzis. Think about your Jacuzzis.

Ask yourself: *What do people ask before purchasing a Jacuzzi? What bothers, concerns, or worries them?*

Maybe they wonder how to keep the water clean, or how to install it. In just a few simple steps you can effectively address questions in a relevant way.

1. Survey your target audience and prospects.
2. Find out what their big questions are.
3. Offer free, accessible answers.

There are many different ways in which you can provide the answers:
» Publish free reports.
» Offer free trials.
» Give away free samples.
» Present demos.

But the ultimate way is to give people the experience of meeting and talking with you.

It doesn't matter whether you're the owner, the *solopreneur*, or if you're selling for a company, what matters is that people get a feel for who you are and what your product is.

To give potential buyers the actual experience with you, try using:

- » Webinars
- » Teleseminars
- » Videos
- » Blogs

All of these mediums allow people to experience the building of credibility and trust. You want to continue the pre-framing and the positioning that you've been doing. That's what you're looking for.

Again, this is all before people are able or ready to consider purchasing anything. People will come in and get a sample that takes them even deeper, an experience that takes them into a place where they're getting so much information and so much knowledge that they're raising their hand even higher.

You've helped them see the results that they're going to get. You haven't been telling them, like a typical salesperson, how amazing, how awesome, and how terrific you are. You're showing them one more time that you're going to continue giving them your great services or products.

People get to see confidence. You will have more and more confidence that they are going to get results from your goods or services when they give you their money.

On your webinar, your teleseminar, or whatever you choose to do, you are continuing to position yourself as an authority, as a celebrity, and an expert. You give away more and more value.

The right client in their magnetized state will eventually raise their hand and say, "I want that. I want that. I want that."

EDUCATIONAL BLOG POSTS

I love using blog posts. Blogs are one of the best things that you can do to attract attention, and to position yourself as a credible expert and authority. I highly recommend you begin blogging immediately.

You can blog by writing, by audio, and by video.

The best blogs are the blogs that make use of:

- » Videos
- » Audio files of those videos
- » Written transcripts of videos

They appeal to all different kinds of people who respond to different kinds of media.

Blogging establishes you first of all on Google as a trusted authority and credible expert. The more blog posts you write about specific topics that your ideal target audience is interested in, the more people become magnetized to you, and the higher rankings that you're going to have on Google.

As people see your blogs, they not only understand your credible expert status, but they also understand more and more about who you are. They understand more and more about your company, your products, your services, even though you're not sharing any of that. You're not talking about any of that. You're simply talking about things that are important for your marketplace.

As an example, in my blog, I talk about marketing. Much of the time I talk about guerrilla marketing, which is low to no-cost marketing. I try to explain the tactics and techniques and share those concepts with my audience.

I write blog posts so the people who read them will have enough information to be able to take action. Because they have learned something practical, people return to the blog to learn more. They want to read it again.

They return to the blog and say, "What's Terri going to teach me today?"

The same is true of the content I share on my radio show.

You can create value through blogging, radio, and many other forms of media and allow people to experience more of your company, your business, or you, as a credible expert. It's all part of magnetizing and knowing, liking, and trusting.

RISK-FREE AND RISK-REVERSAL OFFERS

Many years ago, I learned to offer products or services that are not only free, but also risk-free. I learned this concept from Jay Abraham. I took a program with him that cost about $5,000.

Jay sold me by saying, "Pay $5,000 and if you don't make $5,000 in a period of time"—maybe 90 days, something like that—"I'll pay back every penny."

I remember looking and thinking: *I'm not sure that I want to spend $5,000 on a program.*

But then I saw that there was this risk-reversal, and I thought: *I have nothing to lose!*

Even if people are not a hundred percent sure that they know, like, and trust you, they'll feel that they have nothing to lose.

They'll think: *Hmm, this might be something that I want to buy. I'm pretty sure that I'm building enough confidence that I want to try this.*

As soon as you include risk-reversal, clients become very comfortable dipping their toe in. As soon as the risk has been taken away, and they can do something risk free, they're comfortable going forward.

In my business I offer a program called *The Ultimate Business Growth System* (http://www.theultimatebusinessgrowthsystem.com) where people can actually learn from me, by video, every single week for a full year, with all my tools, resources, templates—everything I've done to create a successful business.

I really want people to go to through this program. It's important to me. So first, I priced it right; but second, I took all the risk away.

It's a one-year program. I allow people to have two full years to decide whether they want it or don't like it and are not happy with it. Even if they get the whole program—no questions asked; they get their money back.

Instead of having a few people sitting on the fence, deliberating over whether to buy, I have thousands of people going through the program. So far, nobody's asked for their money back.

The point really is that when you take away the risk, it brings prospects to their comfort zone.

That's when they turn over their money, and say, "I want to work with you. I want to buy your products or services."

You're not selling, you're magnetizing, in a truthful, honest, integrity-filled way, and you're willing to give people back their money if they're not happy with their investment.

When you allow people to try things risk-free, they instantly say yes. They won't have to think about it, debate about it, or be concerned about it. They'll just move forward, which creates a lot of ease in your business.

NO MORE DEFLATING, NO MORE POSING

A lot of what people do in business (especially those who are spiritually conscious and transformed and who provide holistic services) is deflating. Deflating is when someone shows up who says they can't afford your rates and you instantly deflate and devalue your prices. You want to help. You don't want to lose a client.

Then you are upset that you can't make a decent living and wonder why the Universe isn't giving you the income you need. I want you to make a firm rule right here and right now and that is that you will no longer work with clients who can't afford your services.

You deserve to be paid for what you bring to clients and those who can't afford your services aren't your ideal clients. In fact, the less time you spend with people who can't or won't invest in your services the more clients who really need what you have and want to invest to get results with you will show up.

Another thing I see people doing all the time in their marketing is what I call posing. Posing is pretending. It is being a phony and a fake. Posers are just looking for the money, to gain another client, to pitch another person, and hook them regardless of whether or not they can help them.

This is why I am telling you to stop remembering what you have been taught about sales and marketing. You don't want to pose. You don't want to deflate. You want to be real and to get paid what you really deserve as well.

To be a Heart-repreneur® you want to come from truth. You want to help people and to serve them. Only accept them into your programs or services if they are a perfect fit, and you can bring them results. There is no manipulation, follow-up or overcoming objections. None at all. You are selling nothing.

Think of it this way: if I offered you a drink of herbal tea while visiting my home because I love it, I think it is a good thing to drink, and you said "no". I would not overcome any objection, push it on you or ask you later if you wanted it. I would allow you to make that decision, and would fully honor and respect your decision. Pretty straight-forward, right?

Take a breath with me and allow yourself to accept that marketing is nothing more than word of mouth, getting your ideal target audience to know what you offer and how to connect with you.

All my consulting clients learn a simple method of marketing to turbocharge their businesses. This is my command, connect and convert model. Let's get into that model now.

Command simply means you command the attention of your audience and get known for the result you deliver. As long as you have

CHAPTER FOUR - SHOW AND TELL

a clear Core Unique Positioning Statement people can understand what you offer and see if it is a fit for them or for someone they know. Make sure you really deliver the outcome and as said earlier that you are "The Only".

The **Connect** part of my model is how you show up with the people whose attention you have commanded. They are missing their goal or there is a result they aren't having in their lives or businesses. Think of them sitting out there on an island missing out on what they really desire. They want to move to another island. The island that offers what they do want.

They may want more love, more money, less stress, to lose weight, to start a new career, to find a romantic partner, to be a better parent, or whatever. You connect with them as the bridge to move them safely to the island that holds what they desire. Your entire business is the boat that moves them to what they desire. Connect means you show them the way, the roadmap and guide them safely as they navigate their journey to the island with their desires.

Convert does not mean selling, manipulating or overcoming objections, so let me state that right away. Convert means you allow them to see the path to get to the island. Then they say they want you to guide them, help them get to the island, and they decide to hire you.

Each of these pieces, command, connect and convert, work together in tandem allowing your business to be found, people to see how you can help them, and then has them decide to use your products or services.

True heart-to-heart relationships are how we command, connect and convert from the place of being a Heart-repreneur®. You will see the more you are in your local community speaking, hosting events, and networking, the more your target audience will find you.

Once you command attention, you simply connect in transparency with integrity and authenticity and allow people to convert themselves if they want the outcome you provide.

THE MORE CLEAR YOU ARE... THE FASTER YOU WILL COMMAND THEIR ATTENTION

In addition to having a Core Unique Positioning Statement you also need to be crystal clear as to who your ideal target market is. What are the demographics of your ideal qualified prospects? What ages are they? What gender/genders? Are they married? Are they parents? Where exactly are they located? What kind of work do they do?

Now look at the psychographics of your ideal qualified prospects. What are their values? What do they oscillate with? What is important to them? What ideas do they get behind? I find psychographics to be very important and let me clarify why.

Let's say my demographics are women ages 25-45, who work in corporate, want to start their own businesses, and they live within 25 miles of Westfield, New Jersey. That gives me some ideas of the audience, yet, doesn't tell me where I'll find them.

In my business, I know my target audience is males and females who are 35-65, who own their own businesses, that have less than 10 employees/contractors, are service-based businesses, who are spiritual, interested in health and wellness, care about the environment, get behind causes, enjoy nature, the beach, good clean food, and might also enjoy wine.

I can actually use Pinterest (https://www.pinterest.com/mentorterri/) (I know you probably think your audience isn't there!), to post and pin boards that have to do with spiritual things, positive quotes, health, wellness, causes, green living, nature, the beach, healthy food recipes and wine, and attract a very large audience.

Some of the people in that audience will also happen to be the demographic as well. If you leave out the psychographics you will be missing out on the information that allows you to easily and effortless find your exact target audience. You won't get in front of them when you join community groups or start your own, either.

The only other thing I need to know to command my audience with ease is to understand the result my qualified prospects are seeking. What is their life and work experience like now? What is not quite right with it? What is their ideal vision and what do they want to have in their lives and work?

Once I understand their problem then I can begin speaking about their problem and helping them find solutions to their problem.

Finally, make sure there are enough people in the niche you have selected. If you pick a market where you can't find groups to join locally to find those people, that should tell you something. It's called a clue.

Also, pick a market where people can afford to invest in your products and services. A client of mine came to me with this problem: she wanted to help yoga instructors make more money and grow their businesses. When I conducted market research to find out what the average yoga instructor in a solo business earned it was clear they could not be a viable target audience.

She shifted to growing the businesses of personal trainers because we found their incomes and businesses were more profitable and that people who taught yoga tended to come from a lack mentality only because they thought money should be given away and not earned.

Personal trainers held that money was a great way to be rewarded for the results they delivered. Please don't take this personally. Just understand that for this client the research we conducted led us to these conclusions.

You must be certain you can find these people in a local networking hub or you must be willing to create your own hub. People who have needs and want outcomes and results usually are in some type of hub.

If you resonate with the people you want to serve, are passionate, excited to work with them, and if you can truly help them, then you are in the right direction. Be certain there are enough of them who can invest in your services and products, be certain there are local hubs for them, and you truly are delighted and excited to work with this niche.

EXPLICIT NOT EXLCUSIVE

What I want you to do is focus all your time with the hubs that your ideal prospects hang out in. You will find, if you are like my clients, that some other niches might show up as well. You don't need to turn those folks away if they are people you can help.

One of my clients only works with manufacturing businesses that need leadership training and consulting. He started a local networking group for manufacturing businesses and .a few other local business owners also joined. One of those businesses was a distribution company that needed help with team building. His leadership training and consulting could help that company and he accepted the client work.

It is important not to be so hung up on the one client type that you don't serve others that you really can help. While most of my clients are coaches, consultants, speakers, trainers, and authors, I also work with dentists, attorneys, chiropractors, holistic practitioners, realtors, mortgage brokers, network marketers, and others who fit my demographic and psychographic, who I know I can get results for.

Focus on the one niche you want to help. Offer them help that is specific to them. Then, allow others that show up, and are attracted to you, to experience you, and see if there is a fit.

For example, I held a live intensive for my hub which was "How to Market Your Coaching Business Like a Boss". I had 39 people in attendance of which 6 were not coaches and had no aspirations to be coaches. Why were they there? They knew that their business and coaching had similarities and wanted to learn from me.

When I offered the opportunity to work with me 4 of those 6 wanted that. I knew I could help 2 of them and they were a perfect fit to deliver outcomes to. Two others didn't fit, and I did not believe I was the best person to help them get the results they wanted. I referred those to other people I knew. I did not reject the two that fit.

Also, notice my live event was called "How to Market Your COACHING Business Like A Boss". I was clear and specific to be exclusive to this niche for the workshop. Specific education or networks for specific groups work best. I did not exclude others, I just made certain my niche was being attracted.

Who are you super excited to network with? Who do you really want to work with? Who can you get realistic outcomes for? You must know the answers to these questions to command your audience.

CLARITY WILL COMMAND QUALFIED PROSPECTS

Ready to get excited? As soon as you answer these questions you will find that because you are clear you will command the attention of your qualified prospects.

Demographics:

Age Range:

Gender:

Location:

Profession/Industry:

Ethnicity:

Religion:

Education:

Marital Status:

Parental Status:

Annual Income:

Their Experience:

What kind of person?

What is their challenge or goal?

What options have they tried to overcome their challenge or achieve their goal?

What has caused upset in their lives and businesses that they are embarrassed about?

How do they know they need and want what you have?

What is causing them to want help now?

Are they committed to transformation at this time?

What keeps them up at night?

What is their deep passion?

What is their ideal vision?

What are they open to having in their business/life?

What is the number one obstacle in their way?

Why and how would their life/business be better with your products or services?

Psychographics:

What are the things they enjoy most?

What are their values?

What are they into?

What excites them?

What are they drawn to?

What do they talk about?

Who is someone they hold in high regard?

What is their mission?

What is their pet peeve?

What do they stand for?

What do they stand against?

What do they love?

What kind of human being are they?

CHAPTER FOUR - SHOW AND TELL

What do they read?

What do they watch on TV?

What movies do they like?

Once you answer these questions you will have a very clear picture of who is in your hub and then you can go find them locally!

COMMAND, CONNECT, CONVERT

The beauty of the connect, command and convert model is that you aren't selling people on your credentials and certifications. You are just telling your story. Your story of your business and your life is why people connect with you.

There is something unique, special and different that makes YOU, you. I am not talking about your skills or talents or the outcome you deliver. I am talking about the brand called YOU!

People will be interested in people they resonate with. People who are aligned. This is why you need to give people a taste of who you are, and be with them heart to heart, authentically.

They want to do business with people who are like-minded and see things the same way they do. If you share similar points of view, then it's easy for them to be called to you or to have you command their attention.

Be certain you freely communicate why you are doing the business you are doing, what you are passionate about, and what you stand for and against. Don't be afraid to push people away. By speaking truth, your ideal prospects who oscillate at your frequency will show up, and will be excited by who you are, and what you offer.

In my business, I share my big WHY. First, I let people know I am sick and tired of fake experts and want to shift thousands of businesses on the planet to heart-based businesses. I am also tired of people struggling in business, when I have had it so easy. I want to help them have a lot of money and free time.

Then, I let them know that most of the money I bring in goes to my foundation: Terri Levine Foundation For Children With RSD (www.terrilevinefoundationforchildrenwithrsd.org). I want my ideal prospects to either resonate with me and my why or to find someone else to help them.

TYING IT ALL TOGETHER

Let's recap. Get known for your Core Unique Positioning. Then, find a local community to serve where you can help people get the results they want. Stand out by taking a stand for or against things that are truths for you. Let people get to know not only your skill set, also who you are, and what you believe in. Be THE ONLY in your niche.

PREEMINENCE

LOVE LOVE LOVE CLIENT FAMILY MEMBERS

Your clients are family. They are not numbers. They are not someone who buys your product or service. They are a client family member who you care about and take care of. Instead of focusing on selling anyone or anything, just focus on loving client family members. I love my client family so much that I do everything in my power to create the best results for them.

I love my business. Most of all I love my client family members. I only accept client family who I really want to embrace, to nurture, and to give my everything to. I love my connection with them and to them.

If you are in the right business, offering the right services and products joyfully, then you will be in love with what you do and who you serve.

Just don't take on family members that you cannot get results for or those that you don't feel you can be in love with. I am not trying to be "woo-woo" here. I am telling you that my experience is the more you love what you do and the people you do it for, the more joyful and more profitable your business will be.

If you love your client family, and the products or services you provide, then it is easy to provide outstanding service, because you want to, and because you care about your client family. You don't have to think about things like customer service - it's automatic in all you do.

Keep in mind that your business serves people who want a result or outcome and that they are paying you for your products or services so you can serve them. You are in business to serve them. Make a commitment now to not only having transactional relationships, but transformational ones. Build your business on relationships and focus on your client family members always.

FOCUS ON YOUR CLIENT FAMILY

One of my earlier coaches, Thomas Leonard, taught me the principle of being interested and not interesting. I have taken that as gospel and am focused on helping my client family and qualified prospects gain what they want in their businesses and their lives. I care. They matter to me, a lot. They are not transactions. I really want to know them on a deep level and to help them.

As a Heart-repreneur® based business owner you must focus on solving people's problems from a place of caring and love. When you embrace a higher purpose like this for having your business, you will be happy, and you will make a great living. If you come from a place of service and you offer your help in exchange for payment, people will buy from you.

Shift your business focus externally and not internally. Really deeply tune into qualified prospects and client family members. Focus on serving them fully.

One of my clients, a business coach and psychotherapist, is very introverted. I mean very. When I first asked her to build a hub she felt this wasn't something she could do. I told her to focus outside herself and to only focus on serving others.

Others are hurting in business, and if she could love them enough to host a meeting about them, and serving them, she would not be concerned about being an introvert. She told me that the first time she put her focus outside herself she felt more like chatting with people because she wanted to help them.

She also reported to me that people were gathering around her and she was attracting them to her. The other thing that happened is that when I had her keep asking herself, "How else can I serve my client family members?" she got some answers and was able to tweak and modify her offerings to give her clients more of the results they were seeking.

Every day be committed to a constant and never-ending improvement. This is the Kaizen philosophy that comes from Japan. If you want to have real impact and transform lives and businesses, you will let making money fall into the background and focus on loving your client family. The money will flow as a result.

Every day I ask myself, "How can I serve my client family in better ways to give them better results?" I get answers and I improve my business each day. I am the champion for my client family's goals, do everything I can for them, and make my focus for them and about them. I improve my solutions for my client family all the time.

I never allow prospects or client family members to buy what they don't need or to invest in what will not bring them results. I also make certain they have what they do need. I believe it is my responsibility to make certain they understand what they need, to offer it to them, and explain how it will help them get to their goals.

IT'S ABOUT TRUST - NOT ABOUT TITLES

I used to think people wanted to hire experts. People were calling themselves experts, gurus, and trusted advisors. I don't believe we need to tag ourselves like this. Prove that you care about your client family.

Get them results with your products and services. They will trust you and see you as an expert. You don't need to label yourself as some self-proclaimed expert. That lacks credibility.

How do we get qualified prospects and clients to trust us? One way is with risk-reversals and guarantees. Another is by advocating for your client family, forming a relationship with you as you care about them, and for them. When you don't let them purchase the wrong thing or too much of something they don't need, and you help and guide them to get exactly what they do need, trust builds.

If you add value to them with more education, more bonuses, more tools, more strategies, more resources, more ideas or whatever will get them their best results, and are focused on their needs, you will find they come to trust you in exchange.

I have a policy in my company that we will give our client family much more than we tell them. We don't make promises. We don't under promise. We just deliver.

Preeminence is about who you are being and not what you are doing. If you are ethical in business and get people the results they want, you will earn their respect and be viewed by them as a credible expert.

You simply show people how your products or services can help them. Then, if they become a family member, you commit to helping them achieve the results they want through your product or service. They will draw the conclusion that you are a trusted advisor or guru. You don't need to label yourself in this way.

When my client family members hire me, they do so because they resonate with my beliefs and trust me to guide them to their results. They can feel that I have their best interests at heart and that I want them to succeed.

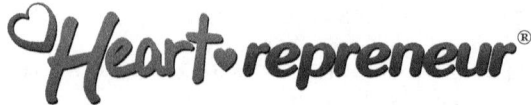

DID YOU KNOW THE HEART-REPRENEUR® TEAM WILL GIVE YOU PERSONAL ADVICE?

As a reader and fellow Heart-repreneur® you can schedule a phone consult with our team. This session is your Turbocharge business game plan. We will go very deep into your business and sort out and solve your business problems. We will expose any overlooked problems and use Terri›s decades of experience to share tools, tips and strategies with you.

Your session will deep dive anything and everything related to your business and can include: lead generation, your online and offline sales process, increasing conversions without selling, your business model, marketing tactics, business operations and anything else business related you choose.

This is a very focused session customized and designed so you walk away with a game plan to fix what isn't quite yet right in your business and will set you up for a great future from a highly regarded business growth strategist who does business as a Heart-repreneur®.

Because you are a reader of this book you can schedule your session now.

If you are serious about turbocharging your business and want Terri's help as someone who has guided the success of over 5,000 other business owners, entrepreneurs and marketers for many decades and believe her real-world experience and Heart-repreneur® style can help you grow your business then grab this opportunity to get a personal consul. This session is yours to ask specific questions, to pick our brains and get advice, information, and knowledge to help you grow your business.

https://www.heart-repreneur.com/new-strategy-session-page

CHAPTER FIVE

• • • • • • • • • •

MAGNETIZE YOUR GROUP

CHAPTER FIVE - MAGNETIZE YOUR GROUP

BE THE AUTHORITY IN YOUR FIELD

The person who is considered the authority in a particular field is the one who people know, like, and trust. Therefore, they're the one that people turn to for information. That's the person who gets the most leads.

Leads come in almost a magnetic way to the authority, because they are the person that even Google will place at the top of the search engine. The same is true with Facebook.

You can become the authority on Facebook when you:

- » Add to conversations
- » Create value
- » Speak directly to the target audience
- » Are well-known and well-respected
- » Are liked and trusted by the target audience

That magnetizes the target audience to want to buy your products or services.

PROVIDE THE MOST CONTENT FOR THE MARKET'S CONCERN

Your target market has major concerns that may keep them up at night scratching their heads, or confuses them in their business or in their lives. It's for that big concern that they're seeking help. They're looking for answers.

They're looking for answers from everywhere, such as:

- Social media
- Blogs
- Articles
- Podcasts
- Videos
- Web forums
- Google
- Stores
- Experts and helpers

Whatever the issue is, you must understand it so that you can provide content and answers for the market's concern. It doesn't matter what it looks like, it doesn't matter what format you deliver it in.

You cannot be an authority, you cannot gain credibility and status with your potential customers, if you don't know the concern that your market has. It's imperative that you don't simply guess this concern. You might be way off.

You should survey your current clients, customers, patients, *and* potential clients, customers, patients. You should ask the questions so that you clearly understand the biggest issue that they're struggling with. Once you understand their big issues, it's actually pretty easy to become an authority in your field.

You're simply creating content that addresses the big issues, takes away the pain, and lets them see that you have their answers. When they buy your products or services, their concern will go away or be completely diminished.

WHAT DO YOU STAND FOR AND AGAINST?

It's very important that you personally identify some core understandings for you and your business:

What do you stand for? What do you prioritize?

What are you passionate about? What do you believe strongly?

You must be willing to stand up and almost shout it from the rooftops.

In my industry, the coaching profession, I've been very vocal and stood up for coaches marketing the way non-coaches market. What I mean by that is using marketing techniques that are used by traditional marketers. Not only relying on things like the law of attraction, and not relying on the process coaches have typically been taught, which is to do complimentary coaching sessions.

I'm very vocal about this because I'm passionate about it, and I believe strongly that coaches can achieve much more financial success if they understand how to market.

You must identify what you and your business have a passion for.

What do you want to stand up and speak up about, even outside your industry?

(Stay away from things like politics or religion, unless it's relevant to your business.)

Is there anything that you stand against, or that you're passionately opposed to?

For an example, I'll go back to my industry. I have a deep "against," which is that there are coaching certification agencies and boards that are determining if somebody gets certified, and it's not an independent process. So, I've not been afraid to stand up and speak against it.

What are you against in your industry?

Again, I recommend staying away from politics or religion, unless those are your field.

Get clear. Be the person who stands up, stands out, and stands against, so that you as the authority can attract the right people.

CREATE A CORE UNIQUE POSITIONING STATEMENT TO ENHANCE AUDIENCE PERCEPTION

A Core Unique Positioning Statement isn't necessarily like a unique selling proposition; a value proposition. It's a statement that, in about nine to fifteen words, sets you apart instantly from anybody else in your field. Think of it as a slogan.

One of the best Core Unique Positioning Statements ever created, in my view, is the one for Domino's Pizza, which used to say, "Delivered in thirty minutes or less, guaranteed, or it's free."

Now any local or national pizza chain could have made that statement, but *they didn't*. Because Domino's claimed that statement, they changed the target audience's perception of how business was done in the pizza industry.

Domino's did something else that's smart. It's the kind of thing you want to do with your Core Unique Positioning Statement. They established their pizza shops right next to college campuses, because they knew their target audience was college students. They made sure that they were right by the campus so they could get the pizza there in thirty minutes or less, piping hot.

With your Core Unique Positioning Statement, you want to understand your audience, and you want to give your audience the instant perception that you do something different than anybody else does in your field.

CHAPTER FIVE - MAGNETIZE YOUR GROUP

You are:
- » The authority
- » The leader
- » The difference-maker

What can you say, do, or guarantee that will differentiate you? What is the industry not doing?

1. Look to industries outside of yours.
2. See what they're doing.
3. See if you can incorporate that in your Core Unique Positioning Statement.

Change your audience's perception, and you will become the authority in your field.

In my experience, the person or company with the highest net profit in their field becomes famous. They rise to the top. They may be nothing today, but they can be famous tomorrow. If you think about how we refer to some products as their brand names, you'll get what I mean.

We call it *Scotch tape* but that's really a brand name for cellophane tape. The name *refrigerator* came from Frigidaire, and some people even refer to it as the fridge.

What can you do to become the authority in your field?

How can you rise to the top and encourage people to know, like, and trust you?

What can you do to make them remember you just like Scotch tape and Frigidaire?

MOVE FROM A GENERALIST TO A CELEBRITY

Businesses start out being very general with who their target audience is. They will work with almost anybody.

Let me give you a couple of examples. I work with a lot of dentists and health-care professionals.

Often, when I ask, "Who would you like to have as patients? Whom should I try to reach on Facebook?"

I get answers like, "Any big case. Anybody who has a toothache. Anybody who needs a bridge."

The truth of the matter is, that's not really who they want.

As we get more specific, I'll typically hear, "No, I want a person who doesn't have insurance, who's willing to pay cash," and then I'll hear more details.

The same is true of me and how I approach my business.

When I first started mentoring and coaching, if you had asked me who my preferred client was, I would probably have said, "Oh, I could work with sales professionals, business owners, people who are in career transition, and I do weight loss," as I did all these things.

But when you're a generalist, you don't get the audience's attention. You don't become the authority, and it's very, very difficult to create celebrity status, to become the known entity in the field, like Domino's.

You must decide who your specific target audience is, only be willing to provide your services to that audience, and only market to that audience. It may be difficult to do, but it will make you the most money in the long run.

PRE-FRAMING

You must get your target audience to know, like, and trust you.

You can do this through pre-framing. This is really a lead-generation strategy. Most people try to get leads by getting in front of their target market, and have the target market engage with them, and then try to sell to the target market. This has become really popular, even with the concept of funnels.

Pre-framing is really different. We don't do it the old-fashioned way, because that actually screams, "Here, I'm going to sell you. I'm going to convince you."

Pre-framing is the right way to go; give people the most obvious thing that they've been looking for, the answer to their problem.

Help people to the point in which they say, "Wow, thank you so much! I'm compelled. You've shown me so much, you've given me so much. You've educated me. You clearly know my problem. You clearly know my issue, and I see that you have my answers."

Through pre-framing, you will find people who are really interested in what you're offering, and they will be attracted as your perfect target market. They'll get something that really helps them. You'll be giving prospects what they want. They'll have confidence in who you are, what you do, and what your business does.

Pre-framing is a form of compelling marketing. It actually sets people up to not only know you, like you, and trust you, but to be willing to ask for your help or want to buy your products versus you trying to drive them into something.

Think of pre-framing as establishing in the mind of your target audience, "I'm here with your answers. I care. You matter, and what I have is going to make a difference for you. I'm not selling to you. I'm giving help, help, help, until you raise your hand and buy." Think of it as planting the seed.

I also call this a form of *reverse marketing*, where the potential prospect is calling or coming to you, versus you chasing them.

WHEN TO BE REPULSIVE AND REPELLENT

Magnetizing is when you:

» Attract your ideal prospect

» Realize you have their answers

» Care about them

» Be the expert

» Become the celebrity in your field

And while that's all very important, at the same time I want you to be able to be repellent and, literally, repulsive to the people that you don't want. You don't want those who aren't going to be served by your product or your services. Choose to reject them, and make yourself repulsive to them.

Let me share an example. For a few years I was doing a great deal of work with attorneys. I didn't choose attorneys; the market chose me. I wasn't pre-framing for attorneys, but somehow, I ended up with them.

I led a lot of workshops, delivered keynotes, and wrote a book for attorneys, but I had not pre-framed attorneys. I had not moved from being a generalist to a celebrity in the attorney field. It became very clear to me that it was because there wasn't a resonance—not between attorneys and me, and not between the attorneys and the products and services I was providing.

I didn't want to attract any more attorneys, and most likely, they didn't want to be attracted to me. Whenever we would sit down and start to build a relationship, it just wasn't the same as with my other clients. I didn't provide the highest value or service for them. So, I purposefully became repellent and a lot more repulsive to them.

I talked on my podcast and wrote on my blogs about why working with attorneys in marketing and social networking was really difficult. In a way, you could almost say, "Oh, Terri, you were dissing attorneys!" I was.

You want to attract and magnetize your ideal client, and at the same time, you want to give repulsive signals to those who are not right to work with you. This will save you time and money. It will also allow you to retain your passion, knowing that you're of service.

Don't be afraid to repel the people you know you don't want and can't serve very well.

INDOCTRINATE PEOPLE TO KNOW, LIKE, TRUST, AND WANT YOU

I use a term that I've borrowed from a marketer named Frank Kern: *Indoctrination.*

Indoctrination is when you inundate your target audience with how much:

» You care
» You understand their problem
» You can bring them fantastic content

Indoctrination gives your clients a sample of the experience you and your business deliver without asking for a dime.

You can do this is by paying attention to what's trending and important for your target audience. Any time you see something that's important to your target audience, or even that's trending on Facebook, help your target audience with information.

You can do this through many different channels:

- Podcasts
- Blogs
- Special reports
- Events
- Teleseminars
- Webinars

A client of mine, a florist, noticed that customers were having difficulty remembering important dates like birthdays, anniversaries, and holidays. Customers would often order their flowers late. So, the indoctrination strategy that the florist and I came up with was to set up reminders. We set up a whole system to make it easy and effortless, so that anybody who had bought even one rose could list the special days that they wanted to be reminded of.

They were indoctrinated just by receiving reminders about the days that had meaning to those customers.

The florist took it a step further by providing additional information with the reminders:

- How to take care of flowers you receive
- How to send the right flowers
- What to send to a funeral and why
- How to send the best precious flowers
- The best flowers to send in springtime

The information was so valuable to the target audience that they began to see my client as not just someone who had a lot of expertise, but also as someone who had great, interesting content that they wanted to receive. They became indoctrinated with my client's philosophy, my client's flowers, and my client's thinking. When the reminders came and it was time to choose a florist, they would buy from my client. The decision was already made for them.

When you indoctrinate, you seal the deal for your target audience knowing you, liking you, trusting you, and wanting you. It is reverse marketing, where they raise their hand to your business.

DELIVER THE MOST GOODWILL

Marketing that pushes and screams at you about how great it is doesn't have a magnetic pull.

The business or company of choice will be the one that:

» Has the most goodwill
» Constantly gives, gives, gives
» Knows what keeps their target audience up at night
» Shows "I care. You matter. Let's make a difference."

That company will attract people who are interested.

When you display these qualities, you attract your perfect market. You'll be helping your market. Prospects will receive what they want; they will once again have confidence. They'll be compelled to come to you, as long as you're delivering goodwill without looking at what's attached to it. It's giving for the sake of giving.

The opportunity is yours to:

» Stand out
» Make a difference
» Become the business of choice

» Become the celebrity in your field

Your competitors most likely are chasing people around using the old formula of yelling about how wonderful they are. We've seen this, a million times. They're thinking that if they just say it over and over you'll be convinced to buy from them. But we know that's not true. It doesn't go that way.

MOTIVATE AND INSPIRE TO CREATE LOYALTY

The goal of a successful business is not just to attract and convert leads; it's to sustain the customers you have. In fact, that's your number one asset: the people who do business with you, and who have done business with you. The goal of having even one new customer, client, or patient, is to create loyalty.

The hidden marketing asset is *loyalty*.

The other day an optometrist said, "Well, I can't keep people the way I used to. They just go to Costco because the glasses are cheaper."

My response was, "If you had created a bond of loyalty, they would not go to Costco to save a few dollars, they'd stay with you."

Your job is not only to attract new people through good will, through being a celebrity; it is also to magnetize the right people. Now, once they become a client, customer, or patient, you'd better treat them like extended family; love them.

By the way, if you don't love them and really care about them, you probably shouldn't be in the business you're in. Think about that. Every single person who pays you anything, you should treat like gold. It keeps them loyal, but it's constantly motivating and inspiring them just the way you did when you were creating the good will to attract them.

Care about your clients just as much as you did in the beginning. Continue to send them information—tips, tools, gifts, cards, whatever it is that shows them how much you care about having them as your extended family member.

Motivate them so that they know that if they went somewhere to save a few dollars, they'd be missing out on what you provide. Inspire them to stay with you by continuing to give, give, give, and giving them all the good will you gave them before they paid you a dime.

Without loyal clients, customers, and patients, you're going to be in a game of hunting, and that's not a long-term business strategy.

EDUCATE, EDUCATE, EDUCATE

In order to attract and keep your ideal target audience, you must create material with information about the things that keep them up at night. Provide them with the information that helps them answer whatever their problem is. They'll know, like, and trust you if you can educate them. Give them the answers to whatever's bugging them by showing them you understand what's bothering them, and you're willing to give them free solutions.

I'm going to give you an example. One of my clients publishes a spiritual magazine. The publisher was working on two major improvements: getting more subscribers and getting more money for their advertisements. But the client was doing it without understanding why the target audience read the magazine, or why an advertiser would really want to be in that particular publication.

They worked with us to offer education about spirituality:
- » They gave away free articles, podcasts, webinars, teleseminars.
- » They sponsored events.
- » They held a free mastermind group.
- » They held luncheon meetings.

They constantly shared spiritual tools. They gave away:

» Meditations

» Photographs

» Drawings

The giveaway was constant. The goal for their readers was singular: Education.

Then for their advertisers, they began to educate them to better understand their target market.

They suggested advertisers ask the following:

Who are these spiritual people?

What has inspired their spirituality?

What were they doing before they became spiritual?

What do they believe?

With whom do they resonate?

What excites them?

All this education showed the target audience had become more attracted to the magazine. There was so much goodwill, there was so much celebrity status, they were so indoctrinated, that the market segment began to pay attention and new customers asked for subscriptions.

The advertisers better understood their market selection so that they were willing to advertise in the publication, knowing that they would be able to speak to their exact target audience, and help them very much. The three words that I say to my clients over and over and over again are really all the same word: *Educate, educate, educate.*

REALLY GIVE A DAMN

Whatever your products or services are, you want to make sure first of all that they answer what your target audience needs; you need to know that you're not just putting out products or services that aren't significant. Your product or service must be something that your target audience truly wants, and that you know they want.

Your product or service must show:

"I care."

"You matter."

"Let's make a difference."

Your product or service must be something that shows that you care so much that you want to help your audience; that you give a damn about them.

Marketing funnels have become very popular. Sellers try to bring in customers with a $7 item, and then a $17 item, and then a $37 item, all the way up. That doesn't show that you actually give a damn, though. That shows to me that you've figured out some sales technique, and that people are probably running away!

Buyers understand when a company or an individual is just in it to get money, just in it to play a marketing game, or are in it to be guru-centric. What I mean by guru-centric is being all about your significance, and not giving a damn about the buyer.

Funnels are the worst approach *ever* in history. It destroys your market. It turns people away because a funnel is designed to get customers and capture them. None of those terms sound freeing and fun and magnetizing, nor do they instill confidence.

Instead, the amount of money somebody's willing to give for your products or services should be in direct proportion to the amount of confidence they have that your product or your service is going to get them the results that you found out they needed. That's how you show that you actually give a damn.

You want to communicate to your customers:

"We can solve your problem."

"We can help you."

"We're here for you."

You build customer confidence not through a guru-centric model, but with a client, customer, or patient-centric model that doesn't care about you and how wonderful you are but truly cares about your customer, client, or patient and their result.

Give a damn!

RADICAL TRANSPARENCY

When you do business without authenticity, transparency and integrity or are in business for nothing but profits people can see through this and won't be drawn to you. For reverse marketing to be in effect and people to flock to you, you must be in business to make a difference for others.

This means all your marketing is done by being radically transparent. It means that you not only keep promises, but you also exceed your client family member expectations all the time. In addition, always treat your client family the way you would like to be treated by others.

To be a preeminent business you must do everything you can to create a bond of trust with your qualified prospects as well as your family members. You will build trust quickly with honesty and transparency.

I remember going back a few years ago when I was consulting with a hospital. The CEO was planning to lay off some people and we were going to be combining some departments to work together on teams. I advised her to hold a town meeting to speak with brutal honesty about the changes that were happening, why they were happening, to invite every single employee of the hospital regardless of their position to be part of the meeting, and to ask any questions they wanted to.

She was very resistant to this idea. I told her that without transparency and honesty, in full disclosure, she would not have buy-in from the employees, and the changes would be detrimental.

CHAPTER FIVE - MAGNETIZE YOUR GROUP

She trusted me as her adviser and decided she would hold the meeting with full disclosure and answer all questions that the employees asked. I told her that if she did not do this morale would be down and the hospital profits would soon follow with a decrease as well. I also informed her that when you are not honest and open with employees, vendors, and others it is very difficult to create any loyalty or trust.

She began the meeting by explaining how much the hospital and the employees of the hospital meant to her and how she was doing everything she could to make the hospital more profitable so the employees could be secure in their jobs going forward. She also explained that the reason she was in healthcare and was the administrator of this hospital was because of her deep desire and commitment to make a difference for patients in the area.

Although she began the meeting with a lot of apprehension about 30 minutes into the meeting she felt the support of most of the employees and how they were coming together as a team to really advocate for their patients and to increase productivity so more jobs could be retained in the future.

I remember watching her shift from fear of telling the truth to someone who was connecting with people heart to heart and really wanting to make a difference. Employees eventually rallied around her and many changes were made within the hospital by employees who came together for the betterment of the hospital and the patients. She developed full trust by being transparent.

I'm happy to report that patient care improved, morale improved, and profitability greatly improved.

I suggest you commit right now to complete truth and honesty when you speak with qualified prospects, vendors, employees, independent contractors, and with your client family. We never need to tell anything but truth to grow our businesses.

Run your business so that people realize it is safe to open up to you or anyone else who works in your company and to be completely honest and transparent. Practice being fully transparent always and encourage others to do the same.

If an error is made in your company, quickly apologize for errors and mistakes and make it up to those that are affected. Take 100% ownership and responsibility of anything that goes wrong. Always do the right thing and you will find that people will come to trust you.

I want my client family to be with me long-term. In every client family relationship, I do whatever I can to maintain that client family member in my life. Don't try to run a business by only focusing on the client member here and now. Focus on that client family member as family forever. This is why I don't want you to be doing business transactionally and instead want you to build heart-to-heart relationships.

By being authentic, excited, and passionate about my business, I attract people everywhere. I have had discussions with people on airplanes who have done business with me. I have spoken to people in line getting coffee who I've later done business with. I am the same person all the time whether I am speaking with a qualified prospect who is likely to become a client family member or with someone that I am having a chance meeting with.

Once a client family member has invested in any of my products or services for any amount, the bulk of my time is spent deepening those relationships. I choose my family members, they choose me and we are a partnership. If I have said yeah to a client family member, I feel it's my responsibility to nurture them, acknowledge them, and celebrate them forever.

This goes to what I shared earlier about the fact that most people do business wrong and spend their time hunting for new qualified prospects. I fall in love with my clients and build relationships with them based on authenticity and radical transparency. I have committed to my marriage with my loving husband for over 38 years. I commit the same way with my client family members and give, share, and support them as I take a commitment very seriously.

I regularly communicate with my client family that are currently buying my products and services as well as past buyers of my products and services. I send them texts, notes, make quick phone calls, message them, and even share with them on social media.

One of my client family members who had massive success with me showed up at one of my events after not working with me for almost a decade. Without asking her to do this she stood up in the room and shared with us her experience of being one of my client family members.

She told how I continued to support her over the last 10 years and was there to lift her up as well as to guide her, that I continued to believe in her, which helped her believe in herself and she believes that is why she has had so much success.

I remember the experience of having her speak to this group and the amount of appreciation that was coming from me to her and her back to me was incredibly energizing for everyone in the room. One of the participants later told me that that was one of the most impactful things he had witnessed and it was why he decided he wanted to work with me. This all transpired in a genuine authentic way and was not preplanned. That's why it created such impact with the audience.

Are your client family members receiving great value by engaging with you? Does your product or service deliver the outcomes that you say it does? Since we only want to create wins for our family members we need to make sure they're fully using our products and services so that we can make a difference in their lives. By giving our client family members a deep, rich, full experience, being transparent and not over embellishing the results they can expect, we will have happy client family members.

Prospects are coming to you because they have a problem and they believe your products and services can solve their problem. You must be radically transparent in letting them know whether or not you can actually solve their problem with your products and services. In turn, do not allow yourself to take their money if your products and services cannot genuinely solve their problem, provide outcomes and/or the results that you promise.

If your product and service makes a difference, you feel great about it, and you feel that you're in a business that really reflects who you are today, then you can market it authentically.

One of my clients was not sure why she was stalling on all her marketing. I asked her if she felt great about the outcome she produced and she said yes. Then I asked her if helping single moms really excited her and was something she still wanted to be doing. Without a moment's hesitation she said, "I'm not really feeling passion for this anymore. I am so into teaching yoga now that I just don't want to devote time and energy to my business."

I suggested that she put her focus into building up a yoga business instead of continuing to serve a target audience that she wasn't enthusiastically excited about serving anymore.

This is what happened to me when I owned my speech and language pathology business. I wasn't very excited about working as a speech language pathologist any longer. I was fortunate that someone purchased my business so I could pursue something that was more interesting to me at the time which was my art consulting business.

I've owned several businesses along the way and worked in corporate America as vice president of marketing for a national company and as president of a national healthcare company. Any time I no longer felt the vibe, and felt I wasn't being authentic in my desire to work in that industry, I made a shift.

Several decades ago I started my coaching and consulting business and often have said I felt at home as soon as I did this. Why? I know myself better today than ever before after spending decades on personal development. I am in love with what I do and with my extended family that I get to serve.

If you are in the right business, then it really is time to begin marketing authentically and transparently.

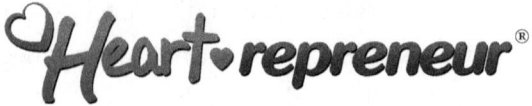

Grab a free ticket to one of Terri's upcoming live events (valued at $1,500!) at https://www.heartrepreneuracademy.com/event-main/

Follow her blog and get more tips, tools and techniques and updated information that will turbocharge your business

https://heartrepreneur.com/blog/

Terri provides free video coaching for readers here:

https://www.youtube.com/user/coachterri

Don't forget to grab your Turbocharge strategy session focused on you and customized for you where a member of the Heart-repreneur® team will give you tips, tools and strategies to grow your business.

https://www.heart-repreneur.com/new-strategy-session-page

Terri looks forward to connecting with YOU, Heart to Heart

CONCLUSION

Where you are in your business can change in an instant. You now have the ability to be more tuned in as a Heart-repreneur®. It's your time to attract the clients that you want to attract, and to do it in an easy, effortless way!

You've learned to use techniques that allow people to flow to you, and allow the right people to find you. You have the ability to position yourself as a celebrity in your field, an authority in your field, and as someone who creates massive goodwill for the people that you're choosing to serve.

You're no longer a typical business owner, using traditional media and trying to convert people to become your clients or customers. You have the opportunity now to begin to create your business and your marketing in a different way.

Commit to notice what's stopping you. Pay attention and see what might be in your way. Go back to any chapter, and use it as a resource. Make certain that you are working in a new way, as a Heart-repreneur®, and that you are no longer marketing the old-fashioned way that turns people off.

Notice others who are marketing in the old way, and how you actually feel about those marketing techniques. You're going to be doing

Conclusion

things differently from now on. Chances are, you're going to grow your business more than ever.

You're going to have a much higher net profit, and you're going to enjoy marketing, maybe for the very first time! You have the opportunity to build your business in a high-net-profit way now, with less stress. You will have happier clients who come to you and want to use your products or services.

You have learned exactly how to work without pushing and struggling, and how to market in an easy, effortless way. Any time something shows up that you're thinking about that gets in the way, or you hear an old sales or marketing myth, just turn back to the chapters in your book, and remember how it is you're going to be marketing now.

You have enhanced your game. You know how to get clients in a new way. Don't let your self-doubt stand between you and the people who deserve your products or services. It's time for you to follow through on what you've learned.

I wrote this book not just to give you some help, but to change your marketing forever, so you wouldn't need another marketing book, so you wouldn't need another business book. I wrote this book because it's been an answer for me and for my clients.

Right in this moment, picture what it is that you want in your business:

- » Visualize it.
- » Feel it.
- » Touch it.
- » Taste it.
- » Hear it.
- » Smell it.

In order to achieve what you want, you have to believe it, and you have to truly be ready to embrace it.

In this moment, you already have momentum. You can set yourself up for success by taking action on what you have learned.

Remember, it's not going to be a struggle anymore. People will happily respond to you and your message. You will have inspired confidence in your customers, because you care about them and take joy in serving them.

Join the Heart-repreneur® Movement now for free and be part of Terri's tribe here:

https://www.facebook.com/groups/heartrepreneurswithterrilevine

Get Access to Terri's Course on Getting Hot Paying Clients here:
https://gethotpayingclients.com/

Watch Terri's free training she put together for you here:
https://www.heart-repreneur.com/master-class/

Get Terri's free tools, tips, strategies and courses when you set up a free account here:
https://www.heartrepreneuracademy.com/

If you liked this book please leave a review on Amazon and also on our Facebook page after you "like" us here:
https://www.facebook.com/HeartrepreneurTerriLevine/

Questions? Contact
james@heartrepreneur.com or call us toll free at 888-776-1124

It's time for you to rock and roll. Get started now and join the Heart-repreneur® movement!

ABOUT THE AUTHOR

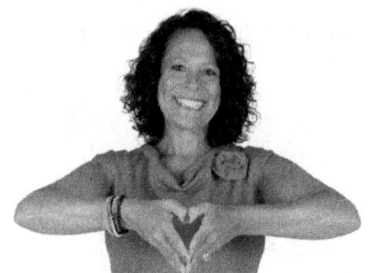

Dr. Terri Levine, PhD

Business Strategist, Chief Heart-repreneur® and Founder of the Heart-repreneur® Academy

She is a best selling author of dozens of books, in demand keynote speaker, and world-renowned business strategist.

Dr. Levine was named one of the top ten coaching gurus in the world by www.coachinggurus.com and the top female coach in the world.

Terri has been assisting businesses worldwide with creating the right inner mindset and outer actions for business growth, has been mentoring businesses for over three decades and helped over five thousand business owners to go from ordinary to *extra*ordinary while having the life of their dreams, doing the work they love, loving the work they do, and being financially secure too!

She has been featured in the media on platforms such as:

ABC, NBC, MSNBC, CNBC, Fortune, Forbes, Shape, Self, The New York Times, the BBC, TEDx and in more than fifteen hundred publications. Her very popular Heart-repreneur® Radio show is

About The Author

downloaded by thousands of people each month https://itunes.apple.com/us/podcast/heartrepreneur-radio/id1159942743?mt=2 and she has begun a new business talk show, TerriTV (www.Terri.TV)

Terri holds a PhD in clinical psychology, is a Master Certified Guerrilla Marketing Trainer and Coach, a Licensed Hidden Marketing Assets Consultant, and a member of the American Institute of Business Psychology. She is a Managing Director of Philadelphia Ambassador for the Evolutionary Business Council, and sits on the board of several nonprofit organizations.

She operates https://www.heartrepreneur.com/, mentoring business owners to create more revenue and profits while learning to be a Heartrepreneur®.

She also has founded https://www.heartrepreneurcircles.com/ and https://www.heartrepreneuracademy.com/.

Terri is also on the advisory board of several companies and dedicates time fundraising for the nonprofit foundation she founded, The Terri Levine Foundation for Children with RSD. (www.TerriLevinefoundationforchildrenwithRSD.org)

If you enjoyed this book, you may enjoy a few of her other recent bestsellers and can find her books at: https://www.amazon.com/Terri-Levine/e/B001IU4TV2.

CPSIA information can be obtained
at www.ICGtesting.com
Printed in the USA
BVHW041036181118
533437BV00014B/307/P